The Tech Intern Blueprint

Ray Parker

with Charlie You

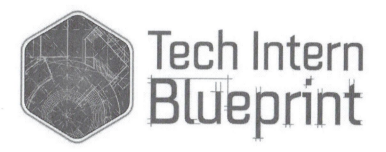

Tech Intern Blueprint

The Step-By-Step Guide to Standing Out, Getting Paid, and Landing the World's Most Lucrative Tech Internships

Ray Parker

with Charlie You

Acknowledgements

Writing this book wasn't very easy. Charlie and I spent far too long getting the content together and figuring out how to add values to readers. Once it was close to done though, it felt great.

I was fortunate enough to have a fantastic team of people who helped me to complete the book and turning it into the form it is in today. A special thanks to Michelle T. and Anton P. for helping me put this book together.

Thanks to Jordan D. and Devon B. for letting me use their personal websites as examples. Ed L., for helping me to refine my resume at the start of my career. Kevin L., for helping me along the way. As well as other friends who have taught me so much during the journey. Thanks to Cara C., Devon B., Dan S. and others for reading through and helping me to polish this book.

To my mentors, colleagues and professional organizations that have helped me to learn so much. To my family, John and Sayuri, Noah -- for motivating me to keep writing for the past two years.

Finally, to my readers. I hope this book helps you on your way to getting the internship of your dreams and the career that you never deemed as possible.

Table of Contents

Table of Contents iii

Introduction vii

Letter from the Authors vii

Chapter Overview x

Author Introductions.............................xv

The Tech Intern Blueprint Core Principles 1

1. Getting job offers is a learnable skill. 2

2. Never give up. It is NEVER too late. 2

3. Consider the company's point of view............... 4

Chapter 1 – Internship Overview 7

What is an Internship? 7

What are the Benefits of an Internship?.............. 10

What Types of Internships Are There? 22

Chapter FAQs and Action Items 26

Chapter 2 – Getting Experience 29

Classes 30

Independent Studies 33

Research Positions 35

Personal Projects.............................. 40

Extracurricular Activities/Clubs.................. 43

Chapter FAQs and Action Items 46

Chapter 3 – Marketing Materials 53

Resume.. 54

Cover Letter.. 69

LinkedIn 73

Personal Website 80

Elevator Pitch 84

Chapter FAQs and Action Items 89

Chapter 4 – Finding Internships 93

School Resources 94

Networking.. 98

Online Resources... 102

Top Tips to Landing That Kick-Ass Internship 108

Chapter FAQs and Action Items 111

Chapter 5 – Applying to Internships 115

Referrals 116

Cold-emailing Recruiters 117

Informational Interview/Cold Referral 118

In-person Meetups... 122

Online Applications 123

Tips and Tricks.. 128

Chapter FAQs and Action Items 131

Chapter 6 – Interviewing 135

Pre-Interview Steps.................................... 138

Coding Challenge.................................... 146

Phone Screening.................................... 149

Behavioral Interview 151

Technical Interviews................................ 154

Chapter FAQs and Action Items 160

Chapter 7 – The Offer **163**

What to Expect..................................... 164

Negotiation.. 165

Choosing an Internship 168

Chapter FAQs and Action Items 172

Chapter 8 – The Internship **175**

Onboarding 176

Aim for Success 176

Make the most of your experience.......... 184

Chapter FAQs and Action Items 185

Conclusion **189**

Chapter Summaries................................. **193**

The Tech Internship Blueprint Core Principles 193

Chapter 1 - Internship Overview............. 193

Chapter 2 - Getting Experience 194

Chapter 3 - Marketing Materials............. 195

Chapter 4 - Finding Internships.............. 195

Chapter 5 - Applying to Internships 196

Chapter 6 - Interviewing 197

Chapter 7 - Internship Offers 197

Chapter 8 - The Internship 198

Appendix **199**

Succeeding at a no-name school 200

Why your sub 3.0 GPA doesn't matter 202

What to do if you're an international student,
minority or disabled? 203

Network your way to 500+ LinkedIn Connections 209

How to position yourself if you're not a Computer
Science major 213

Finding housing and moving across the country .. 214

How to move from one department to another at
the same company 216

Differences in the full-time job search.................. 218

Optimize your career for success.......................... 219

Taking full advantage of the internship 224

Online Resources **231**

Notes **233**

Introduction

Letter from the Authors

Welcome to the Tech Intern Blueprint!

We'd like to thank you for purchasing this book. You've taken a big step towards breakthrough success in your college career by saying "yes" to this process. This is going to be a fantastic experience, and we can't wait to share it with you. We look forward to being able to guide you every step of the way through the internship process and are excited to hear all about your success stories at the end.

How did this all come about? Well, back in 2016, Gallup conducted a poll asking 70,000 college students if they thought their universities' career services office was very beneficial. Their response? Only 16% of the students said it was helpful to them. A lousy 16%, which is not illustrious considering how many college students rely on the services provided by such an office!

This is the reason why we wrote this book: we want every student have access to the information that will enable them to start off their career in the best possible way.

Upon entering college, neither of us had a clue on how to get a great job. We only knew that obtaining an internship was the first step on the path to a great career and we had the intense desire to make it happen no matter what. Whether by skill or luck, we ended up connecting with those who knew how. We became their students and tried to learn as much as we could. Through our own application of this knowledge, we took their techniques, refined them, and created a system that we have since taught to many of our fellow students.

This book covers everything that we know about how to land the best, most competitive technology internships in the world. We are presenting a complete, repeatable, and systematic strategy that will maximize your chances of landing your dream job. If you work hard and follow our advice, even when it seems counter-intuitive, we can guarantee that you will see amazing results.

Before we dive into the details, the next section will give a brief description of each chapter. If one happens to draw your interest, feel free to jump to it and read it on its own. However, we do recommend that you read the book cover to cover at least once in order to best understand the material.

We look forward to sharing our research and supporting you as you take the first step in your journey to a successful career in tech.

Here's to your future!

Cheers,

Ray Parker
Charlie You

Chapter Overview

Through a simple step by step process, the Tech Intern Blueprint will guide you through the intern process and teach you all there is to know about finding, preparing and securing an internship. It will shed some light on some of the more confusing aspects and break it all down in an easy to follow format. We won't be covering how to be productive during your daily life, nor choosing the right career for you, but instead we will help you with the process to get where you want to be. It will inspire your confidence in the process and have you interview-ready at all times. All you have to do is say yes!

We endeavor to leave no stone unturned in our research and explanation. Here are the chapters we intend to cover.

The Tech Intern Blueprint Core Principles

We will begin by discussing the core principles this book is based off of. Keep these in mind while reading through the rest of the chapters.

Chapter 1 - Internship Overview

The first chapter of the Tech Intern Blueprint breaks down the subject of internship giving you a comprehensive explanation to details its exact purpose, what types of internships there are, and the benefits to you as a student.

Chapter 2 - Getting Experience

We discuss the classes you should take and any independent studies and research that is useful for your future career path. In this chapter, we identify personal projects, extracurricular activities and clubs which are suitable for you to lay the solid foundation that you will need to become competitive and differentiate you in a crowded job market.

Chapter 3 – Marketing Materials

Being successful is a direct result of being organized. In this chapter, we discuss resumes, cover letters, personal websites, elevator pitches, the importance of having a LinkedIn profile and the best tips and tricks to succeeding. We will provide you with the absolute best resources to getting started and getting noticed.

Chapter 4 - Finding Internships

In order to find internships, you need to make use of every resource at your disposal. This includes school-based resources, online resources, networking events, career fairs and job boards. We will take you through the best ways to succeed in finding those hidden gems.

Chapter 5 - Applying to Internships

This chapter will walk you through the various methods of applying that exist. We discuss the subject of referrals, cold-emailing recruiters, online applications, networking, and in-person meetups.

Chapter 6 - Interviewing

We remove the uncertainty from the interview process and delve into interviewing, particularly behavioral and technical interviews. We will debunk the myths and give you the resources you will need in order to be successful during those technical and behavioral interviews.

Chapter 7 - The Offer

It's not just about accepting the first offer that is directed at you. This chapter enlightens you on what to expect from your offer, how to negotiate for what you want and finally, how to choose the right internship for you.

Chapter 8 - The Internship

In the final chapter, we will work with you to set your best first impression and rules to keep in mind when starting your internship. We will cover the onboarding process, habits to retain during your internship and how to get a return offer!

Conclusion & Chapter Summaries

The core principles are brought in to conclude the guide and each of the main points from each chapter are summarized.

Appendix

As an added bonus, we answer some of those more common questions we get, including how to network your way up to over 500+ LinkedIn connections, what to do if you are an international student, how to find living accommodations, move across the country, and much, much more.

Online Resources

Throughout the book, we will refer to various templates and worksheets that we've created. By downloading and creating them, you will significantly increase your chances of success. You can download all of these at the following URL:

(www.internblueprint.com/resources)

Author Introductions

Ray Parker

Ray Parker is a Data and Artificial Intelligence Consultant at Microsoft Consulting Services. He studied at Rensselaer Polytechnic Institute (RPI) in upstate New York, where he got his degree in chemical engineering. During his time in college, he did over six different internships including three summer internships, two co-operative education (co-op) internships, and a couple of part-time internships.

When Ray was a freshman, he wasn't sure how to apply for internships, excel during interviews, and snag those sought-after internships that he had heard could boost his career. He struggled to gain interviews and had a hard time developing professionally. He turned to as many different types of resources as he could lay his hands on, whether it was the internet, blogs, articles, career centers, to get those interviews and secure those internships.

Through trial and error, hundreds of hours and thousands of applications later, he landed his first internship at NASA. With his first internship in the bag, he knew that it would be much easier to get a second one. As time progressed, he was able to learn many skills and techniques from all the hiring managers and recruiters that he interacted with. This helped him, in turn, validate the different hypotheses and strategies he had been formulating in his mind.

He spent hundreds of hours refining his techniques and learning as he went, skipping many Friday night parties in the process. And it paid off for him! Through his constant desire to educate himself and the refinement of his knowledge, he was able to teach other peers and colleagues the art of securing quality internships.

During Ray's time at Rensselaer, he was able to earn over 200+ interviews at top Fortune 500 companies and received over 30+ offers as a result of the interviews. And when it came time for him to apply for a full-time position, he had over five offers to choose from!

Throughout his internship career, he has been fortunate to work at companies like the National Aeronautics and Space Administration (NASA), Bristol-Myers Squibb, Orbital ATK, Northrop Grumman Corporation, RainmakeMe Venture Capital, and Booz Allen Hamilton, in various fields including chemical engineering, aerospace, pharmaceuticals, management consulting and venture capital.

Charlie You

Charlie You is currently interning at Amazon in software development. He is an investor at Contrary Capital and is a junior in Computer Science and Math at Rensselaer Polytechnic Institute (RPI). Previously, he was on data science teams at both Workday and Haystax Technologies and has been involved in three different startup organizations.

Charlie knows that without the aid of Ray and their mutual friends, he would not be where he is today. When he entered college, he knew that getting an internship was vital, but like Ray, did not know where to start. Charlie attended a career fair with a poorly laid out resume and an even worse fitting suit. Needless to say, he was unsuccessful. He applied to a few places online but had given up all hope that getting an internship in his freshman year was even possible. But then he met Ray a month later… and the rest is history.

He showed him the value of never giving up and that it is never too late to send out those applications. Ray helped Charlie refine his resume, and he got to work applying to over one thousand companies online. He ended up with three interviews and two offers as a result. Since then his success rate has gone through the roof with 30 interviews under his belt and ten subsequent internship offers.

In the two years since then, Ray and Charlie have had hundreds of hours of conversations crafting theories as to what would make them more attractive candidates for these positions. They tested and refined their methods and out of their countless hours and discussions, created their blueprint.

Now it is their turn to assist you. Through the benefit of their expertise, you too can land internship offers from the world's most selective companies. The methodology they cover in this book has been field-tested in countless job applications, interviews and resulted in full-time offers from some of the leading companies in the world. Together they have assisted many of their close friends and colleagues to land tons of internship offers from well-known companies, which have gone on to convert into full-time positions.

The Tech Intern Blueprint Core Principles

In our own journeys to mastering the process of getting internships, we've noticed a few general themes that kept popping up over and over again. These don't fit in any one part of our system, but rather they underlie everything in the chapters ahead. We recommend that you keep these in mind as you read and especially as you take action on our ideas.

The Tech Internship Blueprint Core Principles

1. Getting job offers is a learnable skill.
2. Never give up. It is NEVER too late.
3. Consider the company's point of view.

---

1. Getting job offers is a learnable skill.

"All business, personal and success skills are learnable through hard work and diligent application, over and over." –Brian Tracy

Most people don't think that getting amazing jobs is a skill that can be improved. They view it as something that is fixed or mainly based on luck. In interviewing our friends who were struggling with this, something that we often heard was "I'm just not good at it, I'm not that type of person."

By assigning your current struggles to your identity, you are doomed to repeat those struggles forever. There is not a certain type of person who is better at obtaining jobs than others. Absolutely anyone can develop this skill, just as anyone can learn to ride a bike or drive. While not all of us are going to be the Brandon Semenuk of getting jobs, with the right knowledge and dedication, you can certainly get to the top 10%.

2. Never give up. It is NEVER too late.

"Nothing in this world can take the place of persistence." –Calvin Coolidge

During my (Charlie's) first year in college, I knew that I needed to get an internship for the summer. I went to my school's career fair with an ill-fitting suit and an even worse resume. Needless to say, I walked out of there with no job prospects and little hope. I knew something needed to change, so I went to the career center. They pointed me to our school's internal job board, gave me a few pamphlets, and left me with this piece of advice:

"Most students don't get an internship their first year, so don't worry if you end up having to wash dishes or serve ice cream this summer."

I followed the pamphlet on resumes to spruce mine up a bit and then applied to a few recommended positions on our job board. Months passed by and I hadn't heard back from anyone. Reflecting on what was said to me in the career center, I gave up trying to find a job for the summer.

Then I met Ray. He showed me that the career center's "advice" was bogus, and that I could, in fact, get an internship my freshman year. He reviewed my resume and made so many changes that there might have been more red ink on the page than black! Ray outlined what was then an immature version of the system that we are presenting now. But perhaps more important than any one tactic on interviewing or applying was his insistence to never, under any circumstances, give up. It is never too late, he said, to get an internship.

During the spring semester, I quadrupled the effort I was putting in to the job search. Over a period of three months, I applied to over a thousand summer jobs. A measly ten of them responded to me with interview requests, and I managed to bomb the first eight. After some more coaching from Ray, I was able to nail the last two and get offers from both, one of which I was even excited to take!

3. Consider the company's point of view

"A change in perspective is worth 80 IQ points." –Alan Kay

Perhaps the most common complaint that we heard from those we interviewed was some form of "I hate it when I don't hear back from a company I applied to." But if you think about it from the company's point of view, you'd realize that they get thousands of applications for every position they advertise and could not possibly incur the cost of both time and money to respond to each one of those people.

This is just one of many things that can be resolved by shifting your perspective to that of a company or its recruiters.

The second most common complaint that we heard was that getting an internship was extremely hard, that even though they did well in the interviews, they were rejected. From the company's point of view, it is much more expensive to hire a bad candidate than it is to fail to hire a good one.

They usually have more good candidates than positions available and thus must err on the side of rejecting anyone who is not shown to be amazing. This is why it is better to focus on being an excellent candidate to a few companies than a merely good one to many. Quality over quantity, we are sure you have heard this before.

You should use this powerful tool when deciding what to put on your resume, choosing what to say during interviews, or negotiating for the salary that you want. In almost every scenario you can gain clarity by putting yourself in the shoes of a recruiter trying to determine if they want to hire a candidate.

With these three principles in mind, we hope that you are able to reframe your own situation and realize that no matter who you are, it is possible to learn the skills that will lead to an amazing job. These don't fit in any one part of our system, but rather they underlie everything in the chapters ahead. We recommend that you keep these in mind as you read and especially as you take action on our ideas.

Now that you know the core principles that lay at the heart of our system, we can share with you the exact strategies that you will use achieve breakthrough success in this part of your life and beyond.

Chapter 1 – Internship Overview

What is an internship? What is its purpose? These are two great questions which are necessary to answer to lay the groundwork for the rest of the book. Understanding their importance will illustrate the fact that any work you do to gain a lucrative internship is both vital and necessary. Consider any work you do from here on in, including the reading of this book and any accompanying homework, an investment rather than a sacrifice.

What is an Internship?

Internships are learning opportunities of varying lengths that students may undertake during a summer break, part-time during a semester, or even as an externship during the winter. They could be as short as one month or as long as six months, depending on the company, your school, and your preferences. The purpose is for you to apply what you are learning in school to the real world.

Don't be fooled into thinking that there is just one sort of internship; all types of companies are involved with internships in some way, shape or form. There are many opportunities available for students of all ages and more than one path to gain an opportune internship experience. Some companies offer direct internships, while others choose to sponsor students. Sponsoring internships makes complete financial sense from a company's perspective because along with a willing worker, they also get tax breaks and other corporate benefits.

If you, as a student, are considering a corporate structure or a big pharmaceutical company, note that not all of these places offer internships. Bristol-Myers Squibb and Pfizer might have internships but some organizations, like Celgene, may not. So, locating prestigious internships with some companies can be difficult for those new to the field. Internships may also come under another name such as the term Research Experience for Undergraduates (REU). For students who are particularly interested in doing academic research or a Ph.D., these opportunities may technically be classified as internships. And this is where much of the confusion comes in.

While internships can undoubtedly be challenging for first-year students to get their head around, they are also extremely rewarding. It is worth taking the time and the effort in following the steps that we cover in the book to land a successful placement. We cannot stress that enough.

It can be an overwhelming process at times. So, here are three things you should know before going into an internship.

1. You're expected to fail – failure is a natural part of life.

2. You're expected to learn new things – both experience and knowledge-based learning will take place.

3. You're expected to grow as a result of your internship – you will be a better well-rounded person because of your intern experience.

And like the companies that offer the internships, not all internships are created equally. You could be assigned to a team or an entire department – it will vary from business to business. There will, in all likelihood, be one specific manager that you have to report to on a regular basis. This will either be the department head or a particular intern coordinator, depending on the organizational setup. Internships are almost always going to be paid. In fact, it has recently become illegal for companies to offer an unpaid internship to students, though many companies do still manage to get away with this. We recommend that you do not entertain the option of an unpaid internship in tech as there is bound to be one that is paid if you look hard enough.

As an intern, you will be handed your own projects to complete which involves a well-defined goal to achieve by the end of your time with the organization.

Throughout an internship, you may find yourself working as part of the overall team, just like you would be if you were employed full-time by the company in question.

At the beginning of your internship, you will be brought up to speed on your given project and contribute to the workload as required by the firm. You will naturally be expected to interact and communicate with others in the organization.

Once your internship has ended, it will be your responsibility to present your work to either your manager or the department as part of your overall assessment. Your internship may or may not lead to work in the future.

What are the Benefits of an Internship?

The purpose of an internship is multi-faceted. However, if we were to answer it in one sentence, we could say that it allows you to find out what you are interested in, make some money and enable you to weigh up your future career options, all within a short period.

Your studies are important; we don't deny that. But, being able to convert that academic knowledge into industry skills will hold you in good stead throughout your entire career.

Gain Real-World Experience

Gaining both the technical and soft skills is not the only way that work experience will help you. You will also be able to make more informed choices about your career when it comes time to choose a full-time position.

While we have found that some students know exactly what they want their role to be in the future, most do not. Within the field of computer science, for example, there are many different jobs you can have ranging from program manager to developer to scientist. Even within each role, there are many different subfields like algorithm theory, machine learning, distributed computation, and many more. While you might have an idea that you want to be a machine learning scientist, for example, you won't know that for sure until you experience it. It is a shame that many students will simply guess when choosing what job to take full-time.

The best way to ensure that you end up with a job that you love is to try various roles and subfields out in your internships. If you find you don't like one or both of them, you are only expected to stay in that position for a few months and you have saved yourself a huge hassle by figuring it out now.

Throughout your internships, not only will you be able to judge what job you are most interested in, you will also be able to find what types of companies you would most like to work for. This refers to the size and the working style of a company.

We define the sizes of various companies as follows: a small company, usually a startup, will have less than 1,000 employees; a mid-size company will have between 1,000 and 10,000 employees; a large company will have more than 10,000 employees. Some of you will like how you know almost everyone and can make a larger difference in a small company. Others will like the established processes and the option to explore the varied departments of a large company. And the rest will like the balance of a mid-size company between the two extremes. We suggest that you try out each company size until you find the one that fits you best.

The second consideration will be the working style of the company: casual or formal. This is most easily discerned by what employees will wear to work: jeans and a t-shirt at a casual one or business attire at a formal one. But the style of a company impacts more than just its dress code, it can also affect employees' mindset on trying new things or how teams communicate. Just like company size, you will prefer one or the other, and we strongly suggest that you try out both.

It is possible that some of you may get lucky and intern at a company that you absolutely love and want to work for full-time. In this case, having been an intern, you have an enormous advantage over the rest of the new recruits: you are already familiar with the company and some of your co-workers, which will enable you to make an impact significantly faster.

Even if you don't like the field or company you interned at, you can avoid those in the future. You now have a much better chance at ending up at a company that you do love working for!

You can locate your passion

An internship will allow you to get some real-world experience in many of the subjects you study in class. Some of you will appreciate more than others. And there will be some subjects you excel in and others that you might like to avoid altogether. Without applying what you have learned and using those skills on a daily basis, it is hard to tell where your particular passions lie.

An internship allows you to put your skills to the test and gives you a better idea of where you might like to work in the future. Perhaps, you are toying with the idea of data science and software development. Having an internship in data science may clarify your like or dislike for the field, enabling you to make a more informed choice.

Being able to have that direct experience can define what you want to do and steer your career path in the right direction. It may even take two or three internships until you find your passion.

You can see which companies suit you more

Having direct work experience in a variety of companies will allow you to try out different corporate structures as well. You could spend some time working in a startup before trying your hand in a large corporation. After your experiences, you can weigh up each opportunity and see where your preferences lie.

You may feel that a large, well-known company is for you and then find that you are struggling with many of the issues that this type of employer brings. Experiment and try different options out while you can, as once you start full-time work in a company, job hopping won't look too good on your resume unless you have good reason. Think of it all as life experience and maximize those situations to your advantage.

You can gain valuable work experience

It is no secret that recruiters like to see prior work experience on your resume. They want to know that you have what it takes to succeed in their company. If you've done well at another company, this will signal to them that you are both technically competent and can thrive in a work environment. These are less common than you might think.

While every graduate of a computer science program will know the ins and outs of the theory of programming, only a subset of those will know how to apply it. And in the real world, application is all that matters. You can know the optimal way to implement merge-sort to avoid cache misses, but that will not help you when you are designing the architecture of a system to use a library component that implements it for you! The heuristics and mental models that you obtain only with hours and hours of practical programming is far more helpful than the knowledge from reading CLRS instead.

Of course, we are not saying to ignore the theory completely (that is the definition of a code monkey), but rather that real-world coding experience is essential when entering the realm of the employed. While there will inevitably be some of this in your curriculum, you cannot beat the experience gained by interning at a company whose software is used by millions of people every day.

Being able to succeed in a work environment is an often-overlooked skill. Some new graduates going into their first job have never worked as part of a team and learned to communicate effectively, had to report regularly to a manager, or even maintained a normal sleep schedule to make it to work at 9 AM! While the transition is easier for many, some will have an incredibly difficult time.

There is no better way to learn this skill than at your first internship. Many employers will give rising sophomores and juniors the benefit of the doubt as they know that this is their first "real" job. Even if you don't nail it perfectly in your first internship, you have a clean slate going into your next internship or first job.

You can grow your network

You can never know too many people. If you have a strong professional network, you will never be out of work and there will always be someone who is able to put in a good word for you. An internship is perhaps the best opportunity in your college career to bootstrap your network. It will be impossible for you to not meet tons of new people even if you are doing the bare minimum.

Any career or work experience will aid you in developing your personal network in the future. If you were to reach out and email some of your contacts in the past, perhaps it would result in a couple of job offers within the week. You can never know too many people, and it is always useful to jot down names and contact information, just in case you need them further down the track.

Meeting new people and making friends is indeed an added bonus of gaining substantial working experience within any organization. Every internship or job you land will introduce you to more contacts. Nurture all the relationships and keep a list by your side. You never know when you are going to need someone to put in a good word for you. Expand your network and build on the relationships every chance you get.

You can get a head-start on those student loans

Perhaps the most visible benefit of an internship is the salary. Many of you will have a significant amount of student debt, and by working for two or three summers as a tech intern, you have a real shot at graduating with much of it paid off! Many loans will defer interest until after graduating, so you will end up saving thousands of dollars in interest if you are able to do this. Never underestimate the power of being debt-free going into your adult life.

If your internship is full-time during the summer, as many are, and you can save a significant portion of it, you put yourself in a much better position going into school. You won't have to get a job that cuts into study time and you won't have to be constantly worried if you'll have enough to feed yourself. This reduction in stress will undoubtedly lead to better academic results.

Another often overlooked benefit of making money is that you can learn good financial habits early in life. Many people going into work for the first time after graduating have never had to manage their own money. They never learned to make a budget and save, but are suddenly making more money than they've ever seen in their life!

This often results in significant over-spending that will cost them later in life. By having money your sophomore year from an internship, you have three years to learn these good habits and can avoid many of the same mistakes when your paycheck is much larger.

You can take those skills to the next level

Taking your studies and practicing them in a professional capacity will enable you to hone your skills and improve on them over and above the level that a classroom situation could provide. Because you will be working alongside other individuals your work will be assessed, and you will be able to pick up tricks of the trade and useful tools as you go along. Companies have standards which need to be adhered to, and any direct experience you gain will upgrade your skills to an entirely new level.

You can secure some references for your resume

Internships are the perfect way to start collecting those references on your resume. With an internship, it is expected that you are only going to be in the job for a short-term, approximately three to six months. It is much easier to change positions and try out a number of different options to get a feel for your niche. And, the larger number of internship positions you land, the more references you can select from.

Securing a full-time job in an unknown company makes it much harder to leave because of the expectation that you will stick around for a while. Internships offer flexibility to climb the ladder, giving you the prompt that is necessary to leap from a small company to a larger well-known corporate entity. Focus on making a good impression to land those future opportunities. Industry contacts will be vital in helping you secure a job and start your career once you graduate.

As a technical major, there are a number of simple things you can do to move up the ladder, get an awesome internship and eventually your dream job.

Step 1:

- Select extracurricular activities or projects you care about.

Step 2:

- Search for academic research and apply skill sets towards other projects.

Step 3:

- Land an industry internship or small company internship.

Step 4:

- Work your way up to your dream internship or where you want to be.

These are the necessary steps that you MUST take to progress along the path to getting where you want to be. Each of these steps will require a lot of time and effort.

Unfortunately, there are no shortcuts in this process, but it can progress you into whatever field you are interested in or whatever company you want to work for. Be thorough and try to locate clubs and activities on campus where you can demonstrate your initiative. This will enable you to find, or come up with, suitable activities and research projects which you can then list on your resume.

You can strengthen your skills on your resume

Your resume might be looking a little thin by now, and that is understandable. Your focus until now has predominantly been on making the grade and getting accepted into the school of your choice. Landing internships is a great way to fast track some experience while studying.

It offers so many wonderful opportunities to build on your skills and demonstrate to other companies that you have what it takes to be an exemplary employee. It also allows you to see things from a new perspective – you will be surprised what you can learn when you are placed outside of the classroom setting.

You can find an employer

You may find that a future offer from an internship may lead to finding a permanent employer. It can and does happen. You may find yourself working for a company who appreciates your efforts, and it is clear that can see yourself positioned there permanently in the future. What enormous inroads you have already made by having some real solid work experience for the company. Note those contacts down because they will prove invaluable in the future.

You can earn some money

Having more disposable cash will help you as a student. However, make sure you understand exactly how much you are going to be paid, as the pay rate for internships does vary dramatically. Of course, even if you do happen to land an unpaid internship, the experience in itself can be its own reward. We won't lie, however, having a wage coming in, no matter how small, is always nice too!

While the money might be great, what is even more important is the experience that you will gain. Depending on the company, you will either have a specific project defined for you, or you might work as another member of the team.

As you can see, there are many notable reasons to apply for an internship. Even if you don't land your first internship at a large company or even the company of your choice, that's not necessarily a bad thing. It will increase your chances of getting some corporate experience and enable you to jump from an unknown company to a mid-sized one. After that, you can make the move to an organization that is perhaps better well-known. If, for example, you had an internship at Google on your resume, how do you think people would react? They would think, "Google doesn't hire inferior people" and you will automatically go up in their estimations. It's an impressive position to be in!

At the end of the internship, you will present your work to stakeholders of your project as part of a final evaluation that will determine whether or not you are invited back for another internship or a full-time position.

What Types of Internships Are There?

Okay, let's get down to specifics for a moment. In the world of internships, terms tend to be swapped interchangeably. Primarily, we are just going to concern ourselves with Internships and co-ops as they are the most relevant to this discussion. Fellowships, research positions, and NSF REUs tend to be aimed at graduates and postgraduates or undergraduates going for PhD's or advanced degrees.

There are six types of internships which can be categorized as follows:

1. Internships
2. Co-ops
3. Externships
4. Fellowships
5. Research Positions
6. NSF REUs

Internships:

Internships last for approximately three months and have a lot of flexibility. They can be done throughout the school year in a part-time capacity, or full-time during the holiday periods. They give students a feel for what it would be like to work in a specific position or industry for a short period.

Co-ops:

Co-operative education programs, or co-ops for short, tend to last for a more extensive period – from five months up to a year, or sometimes even longer. Students wishing to partake in a co-op will have to stop taking classes to work full-time for an organization.

Externships:

An externship is a temporary program which can last up to two months. It is essentially a job shadow, where you follow a professional's movements for a nominated period of time and see what their job entails. This type of position is suitable for any level.

Fellowships:

A fellowship lasts for three months or more and, like a co-op or internship, they accelerate the path to better career options. They are usually offered at a graduate or postgraduate level and can differ in terms of their responsibilities and eligibility depending on the type of commitment it is.

Research Positions:

Research positions are offered at the undergraduate and graduate level and are three months, or sometimes more, in length. Depending on the professor and funding.

NSF REU:

The National Science Foundation Research Experiences for Undergraduates (NSF REU) allows students to get involved in research projects at their institution. Stipends, as well as rent and travel subsidies, are provided. An REU is three months, or sometimes even more in length, and is available to graduates. REUs are very tech specific covering Biology and other scientific disciplines. There are also many different opportunities for individuals in data science and bioinformatics by way of REUs.

Whichever type of internship you undertake, your confidence in being able to perform well under pressure in a professional environment will increase, and you will be able to grow your network profoundly. As you can see, the benefits of doing an internship include more than just a paycheck at the end of the month.

To conclude, we'd like to introduce you to the concept of the career ladder. The rungs on a ladder are meant to be climbed on at a time. Sure, it is possible to skip one or two at a time, but it is difficult and you may end up falling off the ladder entirely! Similarly, in your career, you should not expect to land a job at Google or Facebook on your first try. Yes, it is possible, but it is not realistic. We would position those companies on the third or even fourth rung, which means that you might have to work for two or three other companies to gain the experience needed before you have a good shot at one of them.

While this may seem like a bad thing, it is in fact very good! I may seem like an impossibility now, but anybody can climb their career ladder one rung at a time, which means that anyone going into college has a real shot at making it to those top companies by the time they graduate.

Deciding that you want to spend the majority of your free time sourcing an internship is a big decision. And chances are, not everyone will understand it. Actually, the reasons may not even be ultra-clear to you at the moment.

Why do you need to spend all those hours researching, preparing, sourcing and applying to all those companies? What's in it for you? Well, the answer is a lot of things. There are many great reasons to do an internship as we covered in this chapter. You will find that things will become a lot clearer as you delve deeper into the book and put some of our steps into practice.

Chapter FAQs and Action Items

Will an internship or a co-op be best for my career?

Well, the answer will depend on what your aims are in the future. If you know what you want to do, then taking a semester or two away from education may not be the wisest choice for you. You may want to consider an internship first and foremost. However, if your goals are a bit unclear and you don't mind taking a semester or two off to earn money and build on your skills, then it is worth looking into a co-op.

If there is a particular field of study you want to try to get into, such as venture capital or banking, taking a semester or two away from your studies will give you some experience and an edge over other candidates. You can build more connections and excel in the field with real corporate experience under your belt. Experience in any form is advantageous, and nobody can take that from you.

What should I be looking for in terms of salary?

The salary will vary, but all in all, you can expect to earn between $15 and $20 an hour if you are interning for the summer between your freshman and sophomore year. Once you have completed your first internship, then you can expect your earnings to rise depending on your experience.

It's not uncommon for upperclassmen to earn around $35 to $50 an hour, and in some individual cases, even as much as $65, or more!

Action Items – 1 Hour

Now it's time to put all the theory into practice using our action items. We hope that you are now convinced that getting an internship is one of the best things you can pursue in your college career. At the end of each chapter, we include a list of actions you can take to implement the ideas we've presented. These are optional, but extremely recommended for you to get the most out of this book.

1.   Create a word document and list your goals and relevant notes concerning where you may want to work in the future. This can be a tangible list of various company names and areas of expertise or industries.

2.   Write down smaller achievable goals that will help you get from where you are now to where you want to be. What do you want to achieve in three years? Where do you want to be in five years? Knowing your goals and creating a plan which includes them is conducive to your success.

3.   In a spreadsheet, list the names of the companies you wish to apply to and any of their relevant details (website, email address, address, telephone numbers, and contact names). For ease, we have created a template which is available below.

Opportunity Template:
(www.internblueprint.com/resources)

Chapter 2 – Getting Experience

Now that you know why we believe that getting a tech internship is one of the best things you can do, we will start to talk about how to do it. The first step in this process is to secure relevant experience. You may not be aware of this fact, but recruiters are heavily biased towards filtering out anyone who could end up wasting the company's time and money. They don't necessarily care about the false negatives, that is, the people they reject who would be suitable for the company. And they rarely give any second chances.

The best way, therefore, to show a recruiter that you do not intend to waste their time is to have some real-world work experience on your resume. It goes without saying that an internship in a relevant field is the smartest way to do that. But, failing that, there are other things out there that recruiters look for to gauge future performance. From a recruiter's perspective, the principal thing to assess future return is for them to focus on past performance and experience. While this can be difficult if you don't have any work experience, consider your classes, personal projects and extracurricular activities as a healthy place to start.

They are vital to getting your first internship and moving up rapidly in the internship process. Having the right experience will lay a strong foundation to moving forward.

In this chapter, we are going to discuss:

- Classes
- Independent studies
- Undergraduate research positions
- Personal projects
- Extracurricular activities and clubs

Each one of these subjects is critical in clinching that awe-inspiring internship that you are here to secure. It is vital that you don't rush over any of the topics and consider each one on their own merit. They will guarantee you gain a solid foundation in which to attract those internships and job offers.

Classes

When registering for classes, think about which particular fields interest you and where your potential internship opportunities lie. This must be at the forefront of your mind before you sign up for any classes. Any classes you take should at least sound relevant to your chosen field or give you skills that you may not be able to acquire elsewhere. As an example, if you wish to consider a Data Science internship, then a class in computer optimization could be useful. Data and Society may sound suitable at the outset, but it could turn out to be of limited benefit in securing the internship. A deep learning class may also be gratifying as it teaches skills that are very relevant to this field.

Taking a class that interests you, has a well-revered professor teaching it, or is something that you are incredibly efficient in, is another excellent strategy. The general rule of thumb is that you should either be putting a lot of effort into a subject you care about or minimal effort into subjects that would look favorable on your resume and cumulative academic performance (CAP) report, also known as your transcript.

In some cases, you can request to sit a final exam for a subject without even attending classes for the semester, and still get the credit for that class. Some schools allow you to have transfer credits. If this is the case, try to opt for as many hard classes as you can via community colleges, high school advanced placement programs or online educators. If your school allows you to, take advantage of these opportunities as much as possible as it can reduce the time it takes for you to graduate.

Overloading the number of credits that you are taking in a semester means that you will have a more significant number of options should a class turn out to be unsuitable as the school year progresses. There is ordinarily quite an extended period from the beginning of the semester before you have to decide whether or not you wish to consider dropping out of a class. This gives you plenty of time to determine whether a course is going to be useful for your career or if you are, in fact, interested in pursuing that particular subject. Additionally, you can weigh up issues such as whether the workload is manageable and if the lecturer is competent. These are all relevant factors which need to be carefully considered when choosing your classes. Overloading allows you to achieve a reasonable course load should you find some classes not worthy of your time. If you decide you no longer want to take a class, then there are no adverse ramifications for dropping it. It is necessary to explore subjects that you may be more unfamiliar with and aren't 100% certain whether you are going to be interested in the topic in the long-term.

Generally speaking, the more interesting classes will have various (and often unnecessary) prerequisites that you must meet to gain entry. These are set by the department or registrar, rather than the professor who teaches the class. Often, you do not need to have all of the prerequisites to get access to these courses; there is almost always another alternative. It is worth speaking to those in charge to see what can be done. Schools will frequently let you have an authorization form from the dean or registrar to allow the professor to permit your entry to their class. Nothing is lost by asking the question.

Meeting with the professor to show your interest in the subject and demonstrating you want to take this class even though you don't have the prerequisites can avoid you taking on unnecessary courses. Occasionally, the professor may quiz you to see if you know the subject. In reality, the tests are pretty effortless to pass, so don't be too concerned about them.

Independent Studies

An independent study project is not a class that you attend. It involves you opting to undertake a more personal project that you're interested in under the advisement of a professor or mentor. Talking to a professor about a startup, research project or paper that you want to work on for extra credit can result in an extra A grade.

Independent study projects free up a lot of credits. Or, if you prefer, they can also use up a lot of credits. Using them as a substitute for an elective class that you would otherwise have to take, can be quite a smart thing to do. These projects can set you apart from the other students. As a bonus, you can apply your particular skill set and turn your personal project into a potential startup or another source of income. Talk about a win-win for everyone!

What continuously amazes us, is that very few students decide to undertake independent studies. This is unfortunate considering how easy it is to create a syllabus by defining a couple of projects you're going to do and then carrying them out. The projects themselves can typically be completed within the first couple weeks of the semester, which then allows you time to focus on your other classes, while periodically submitting parts of the project to your professor.

Being able to plan and carry out a project is one of the key things that we'll address in more detail. But let's just say at this stage that if you intend to undertake a personal project, then you must do all that is necessary for your professor to sign off on it.

When listing your classes on your resume, you need to keep in mind that everybody else has done those same classes as well. Therefore, it is essential that you digest and differentiate yourself in some way. Often employers look at the skills you can showcase, rather than the actual classes that you have taken, or the actual grades for those classes. Fortunately, if presented well, you don't necessarily have to do well in a class grade-wise to get an internship in the field of your choosing. Being able to demonstrate the skills that you have gained from these classes, even if you didn't get an A, is the most relevant factor here. Technical employers do not care what your grades are, as long as you have the necessary skills, as well as the inclination, to do whatever the internship entails.

Consider for example that everyone who undertakes a Computer Science I course will be able to use Python. Now weigh that ability up against a student who applies that knowledge to an independent study. Through that one smart choice, that student can show to a prospective employer how they have effectively used that skill in a real-world setting. They have managed to set themselves apart from the others and be immediately more attractive to those who are hiring. If you are allowed to give a name to your independent study, even better. It will then stand out on your resume as something original. If an interviewer decides to query you on your project, you can use the conversation to your advantage and demonstrate your ability for innovative thinking.

As you work your way through the world of academia, you will soon learn it is very abstract. A lot of professors have very little idea of the applications of their subject in the outside world, and sometimes they offer up very outdated information. It is up to you to decide where and how you can apply this knowledge and ensure it is applicable to your circumstances.

Research Positions

Research REUs and URPs can come in a variety of forms and are extremely viable as they aren't as selective as a lot of other internships at places such as Facebook, Microsoft or Google.

REUs and URPs are one of the first key steps to gaining a high-end interview or internship at a big tech company, yet often they are overlooked. From our experience, they are the quickest route to enter a grad school. In most cases, REU research is predominantly what they look for in their applicants. They may not even be interested in other internships that you have done. All they care about is the academic progress you have made at your REU or your research experience at your university. If you do decide to undertake an REU at a specific school, it is almost guaranteed that you will get a PhD offer from that school as well.

REUs and URPs can secure your name to publications, as well as cement valuable connections with many different professors who might be taking your classes. A lot of PhD candidate connections can develop here as well, as many of the professors eventually go on to high-end, assistant research professorships and tenured track professorships. You never know where they're going to end up and how advantageous they may be to you in the future. Consider everyone you meet as a valuable contact and treat them as such.

Many professors often specialize in one area so fostering a connection to a particular professor, particularly one that is world-renowned in their industry, is invaluable, not to mention looks pretty distinguished on your resume. A professor may have a treasure trove of connections. You never know who they may be connected with; let alone the companies they can open doors to. Besides, it is a marvelous method to gain a lot of hands-on experience and skills that apply to a variety of different internships. Developing close relationships with professors is going to support you if you require letters of recommendation for entry to grad school or into other internships later on.

While your interest may not lie in a research lab in the long-term, the skills you obtain during your studies could lead you to secure a co-op or internship at a company in the future. Learning is invaluable, whatever the route, and you can never underestimate the worth that a company may see in your research positions.

REUs and URP give a substantial indication of what academic life will be like in the future. Consider it a real-life trial if you will. Even though we are mainly focused on tech internships, depending on your chosen field, much of the subjects are very closely related. For example, the field of bioinformatics is very tech oriented, and it gives you a generous insight into a lot of different areas which you can then use to direct your career path.

Using undergrad research to stand out cannot be recommended enough. Professors will advertise for undergrad researchers and surprisingly get nobody in return. Very few people realize that doing research, especially for credit, is hardly any work, for a very manageable A grade. These projects can even result in you getting your name on a paper, which unquestionably makes your resume stand out from the others, especially if you're working in a field where there are very few publications and slight competition. Meeting with professors during their office hours and showing an interest in whatever research project they are working on, can often result in an undergrad research position.

Another way of gaining entry into a project is to do your research thoroughly beforehand. Go to the faculty research website and read up on what kind of projects individual professors are working on. You can then write them an email introducing yourself, and letting them know you found their research of particular interest. You can then go on to mention the specifics of their project and classes that you've taken with them. Your main aim here is to try to demonstrate your understanding of their project. At the end of your email, ask to set up a meeting with them to see if they have any potential research opportunities available. Sometimes, professors will get back to you about a meeting, and then if they have a position available, they'll assign you to a grad student that you can then do your research under.

It's prudent to accept URPs for credit rather than money. If you get it for credit, it will go on your resume as a real class and will be more cost-effective in the long run. If you do it for money, you have to work approximately 10 hours a week for 10 dollars an hour. It hardly seems worth it! The equivalent credit-hours are going to be closer to around $100 an hour based on how expensive your college is. Keep in mind that you can always get money later on; but you can never change your grade point average.

As a research project will gain you experience, credit and potentially a well-known name on your resume, there is very little reason not to consider it. While not all research projects will apply to your study or even be practical in your circumstances, they will assist you in one way or another. Extra credit, skill sets, and contacts are worth the consideration.

If you are a freshman, or just trying to fill out your resume, undergrad research will give you a remarkable edge. It makes you come across as more highly skilled and employable than the rest of your classmates, which is precisely your end aim.

Undergraduate research projects or URPs are university specific. Rensselaer Polytechnic Institute, as an example, will pay you a small sum of money in exchange for a research project that you carry out, document, and then allow you to present your findings under the supervision of grad students. As RPI is a predominantly research-centered institution, the professors are highly focused on their own research projects. Being research-based has many advantages and disadvantages, but should probably be a predominant factor for individuals who want to pursue a PhD, or enter a career in research or education. This can literally make or break your resume depending on your goals, or it could potentially set you up for a specialization within a given academic field.

As we mentioned earlier, REUs are the most direct path into academia and can even replace internships during the summer if this is where your field of interest lies. Usually, they will have everything planned out for you in advance. You will find that the REU programs will quite often pay you well and give you a lot of additional benefits such as on-campus housing, a stipend and access to buildings such as the gym, etc. As a bonus, REUs can potentially turn into more academic opportunities in the future such as conference presentations or papers. So, while it may look similar to a summer internship at the outset, it can offer more benefits to a student down the track - particularly one who is focused on going for a PhD.

When you apply for an REU position, you need to be organized. Make sure you have these things prepared in advance:

- Letters of recommendation
- Personal statements
- Samples of your current research experience
- A list of what you are interested in

If you are interested, then we recommend that you log on to the National Science Foundation's Research Experience for Undergraduates page and start looking at the various positions and applying for the ones that appeal the most. Many of these applications are due around January and February, with some due in December, so make sure to get started early on your applications. Getting into an REU at a particular university will almost always automatically lead to acceptance into a PhD program later on

Personal Projects

If you are not able to secure a project for credit through an organization or an independent study through a professor, then you still have this avenue available to you. Personal projects or independent studies will further develop your skills although they are unable to be accredited to your qualifications. If you are seeking a personal project to gain experience or demonstrate your talents, you might want to consider Open Source. Remember, however, that the project you settle on should reflect your passion, regardless of whether or not it is relevant to your chosen field.

From a software perspective, Open Source allows you to promote yourself and your brand. It will also help you gain incredible technical skills, especially if you post it on the development platform Github and blog frequently about your progress. Open Source is a wonderful way to contribute to, and collaborate on other people's projects and will build up your necessary skills to secure an internship. Rensselaer Center for Open Source (RCOS) is one such center located at RPI.

So where do you start? Well, consider making a list of software products that you wish existed. Whether anyone else wishes to use the product is irrelevant. Once you have your idea in mind then developing it through Open Source makes ideal sense as you can put it on your resume. Blogging about it on your website opens more personal marketing opportunities which we will cover later on. And if it happens to be something that others wish to use in the future then you can improve on it at that time.

Contributing to an established project is the second option. Doing so successfully will showcase your skills and be a huge resume booster. You don't have to create the project for it to benefit your career as long as you can establish with clarity that you were able to assist.

Not only will a personal project consolidate your skill set, but it will also provide you with some worthy talking points for your interviews. Being able to talk about previous experience in an internship or the fact that you successfully committed to a long-term project, will market you spectacularly. It will differentiate you from all the other candidates in future interviews and enable you to talk about a project you are passionate about. It will put you at ease during your interviews and give you a real opportunity to sell yourself. And don't ignore the fact that all of these experiences you create for yourself will develop skills that are applicable in any field. That in itself is extremely invaluable. And if a project does happen to be relevant to one of your classes in the future, then you may be able to submit some of your work and gain credit for your efforts. And remember, your idea could potentially turn into a startup or a subsequent income stream. Just try not to limit yourself; one opportunity could open up many doors and benefit you in areas you never even imagined.

Finding the time to work on a personal side project can be difficult. It will all come down to your ability to effectively manage your time. You just have to have some discipline to try to find a couple of hours a week that can be dedicated to your project.

Here are some tips that you can implement right away to ensure you have more time up your sleeve.

- Skip those Friday night parties. They are not a priority.
- Schedule your project into your timetable, so it is not forgotten or pushed to the back of the queue.

- Stop multitasking. It can actually cause you to take twice as long to complete your tasks.
- Write lists so you don't have to spend time trying to remember things.
- Make sure your plans are realistic. Only allowing a few hours of quality sleep is not practical in the scheme of things.
- Minimize procrastination. When you notice you are doing it, then do something about it.
- Be flexible. Things can and do go wrong so ensure that you have room up your sleeve to reschedule as necessary.

It is achievable; you just have to make it a priority. And those sacrifices you make today for your independent project will result in future benefits down the line.

Extracurricular Activities/Clubs

Fortunately, there are a lot of extracurricular activities and clubs on campus that you can participate in. In fact, you may even be spoiled for choice! Consider adding at least one point of value to your resume per semester to make paying your tuition worthwhile. Whether it be winning a business plan competition, or getting a new leadership position in a club or sports team, these activities will guide your resume and showcase the wide variety of skills you have. It is also a smart way to develop your interests, seek out new ones and meet like-minded people. Through the people you meet in the various clubs or activities, you may even be able to collaborate or identify personal research projects that interest you.

Even if socializing is not at the top of your priority list, it is necessary that you go to conferences and get to know your upperclassmen. They may be able to supply you with ideas and opportunities and refer you to internships that are vital to your college experience and career. In addition, finding a mentor or being able to tie your extracurricular activities to your research projects or independent studies is a subtle way for you to figure out how to showcase your leadership and community service activities.

Whatever activities interest you, seek them out. It is a clear-cut method of achieving the necessary experience to get an awesome, well-paid internship. Joining a fraternity or doing community service on campus with Circle K or Alpha Phi Omega, two service organizations, are ideal to find people with similar interests and can develop your social life. Once you finish your time in the freshman dorms; groups start to separate out. Joining clubs and activities at the beginning can solidify your personal life and what you do outside of classes on a regular basis during college.

Social life aside, there are a large number of other benefits to joining fraternities. These groups often have large networks outside of college, which can provide you with valuable links to various industries. Most chapters hold a book of graduates, where they work, and their contact information. This is another brilliant method to get your foot in the door, land a couple more interviews, or get your resume passed on to someone in your chosen field. It can be seen as another leadership opportunity if it's something that you feel passionate enough about. Gaining leadership experience early is essential to succeeding in internships and progressing in your career, and it looks spectacular on your resume too! Eventually, you're going to want to step up and lead other people, so bear that in mind when you are trying to figure out where to spend your time.

If you are interested in a particular club or subject and it is not represented at your school, you can always start one up. While most people tend to shy away from this as it sounds like a lot of hard work, it is not as difficult as it sounds. You will need to meet with a faculty adviser who can advise you on what you need to do to start the club. Then you schedule an interest meeting to see if there are enough like-minded individuals wanting to attend. If there is, you are automatically made the president which is a noticeable title to have on a resume so early in your student career.

The final way to get involved in a valuable activity is through a sports club.

Involvement in sports has many benefits:

- You can meet people with similar interests.
- You can stay healthy and fit.
- It acts as a superb way to relieve stress.
- You can improve your time management skills.

- You demonstrate your ability to work as a team to future hirers.
- It can develop your confidence and self-esteem.
- It can give you a mental break from your coursework and personal projects.

If you can be nominated as the leader or captain of your sports team, do so. However, make sure that it doesn't take up too much of your time unless you're a school athlete, as you need to fit in those personal and research projects to enhance your resume.

Additionally, don't forget to consider the fact that if an alumnus graduates from your school, you can reach out to them purely because they played the same sport as you. This creates an automatic connection even though it has nothing to do with your professional world.

Chapter FAQs and Action Items

What is an acceptable Grade Point Average?

First, let us say that we get this question all the time. In the grand scheme of things, your GPA literally does not matter at all, unless you are looking to get into grad school or a PhD program. One of the great benefits of being in the tech industry is that many employers will not filter you out based on your GPA. Of course, all things being equal, a 4.0 is better than a 2.5. But things are not equal: most often a 4.0 student has less free time than 2.5 student. If the 2.5 student uses that time intelligently by pursuing more real-world experience in the form of part-time internships and personal projects, he will be in a better position than the 4.0 student.

To make this more concrete, we suggest that you try to be as efficient as possible in your schoolwork. For the subjects that are relevant to your future, you should put in the maximum effort because it will pay off later. But for those subjects that are not as relevant, you should try to maximize the grade to effort ratio. For some, this will result in a near 4.0, for others, a 2.5.

Do not worry about the number, only worry about your efficiency. Skills are so much more important to have. If you follow what we teach, then you will be successful regardless of what your GPA is!

We will not go into specifics on how to maximize efficiency, but we can point you to external resources. The two that have helped us the most are the blogs of Cal Newport (www.calnewport.com/blog/) and Scott H. Young (www.scotthyoung.com/blog/).

Finally, note that the above advice on GPA goes out the window if you are planning to apply to competitive graduate schools. In that case, you will want the highest GPA possible.

What skills are the most beneficial to learn?

There are three things you must learn to further your career:

1. Soft skills

These cannot be learned overnight. There are many soft skills which could be helpful for your career. These include public speaking, communication, teamwork, problem-solving, critical observation, leadership and self-motivation. Always keep an eye out for ways to work on these skills.

2. Technology

Undoubtedly technology is going to be a huge part of your career, wherever you might end up. Every single field of study and industry nowadays is affected by technology; nobody is safe. We are living in one of the most technologically advanced times in the history of humankind, and it is such an exciting time to be alive.

That being said, things can change instantly. Keeping up with technological advances and having baseline skills and understandings of programming languages, such as Python/R, and knowledge of new technologies such as blockchain, as well as other skills that you might not think would be applicable, may turn out to be innocuous to your success.

3. Hard skills

Hard skills can be built on throughout your studies and even long after your career has commenced furthering your prospects. These will vary depending on your focus but can include skills such as relational databases, business analyst techniques, algorithms, etc.

If it doesn't fit into one of these three categories, then you can assume that it probably isn't worth learning about.

Getting experience is all about laying the necessary groundwork to succeed in all the other aspects of getting an internship. It can improve your networking prospects and allow you to figure out where your interests lie. After all, how can you possibly know what you are interested in if you have had no real experience in the field? Thinking you may like something and knowing it after you have done an internship couldn't be farther apart. We can assure you that you don't want to be that person that makes assumptions throughout their career as you may find yourself bitterly disappointed.

Most people just don't get the necessary experience to get an internship that will develop their career. If you don't get an early start, then it can seriously affect your internship search later on throughout your college years. Always remember that the groundwork you do today, tomorrow and next week is an investment towards your future. Once you land that first internship, it will be much easier to get your second and third, and eventually a full-time position.

Action Items – 1 Hour

We hope by now you feel a bit better about your current situation. As you can see, even if you don't have experience at the moment, it shouldn't take you too long to find something that will stand out on your resume. Scout out those extracurricular activities, research experiences, personal projects and clubs and determine what the best ways to spend your time are. As we talked about before, it all depends on what you want to do. Once you have analyzed your potential opportunities to shine, it is now time to learn how to put the materials together so you can benefit from the decisions you have made.

Many of the decisions you make now will affect your career options, so weigh them up very cautiously. These three to-do action items will ensure that any classes, projects, clubs or activities you choose will move you in the right direction.

1. Go through, reevaluate all of your classes and make a new schedule according to the process we provided in the first section. Amend your existing schedule accordingly.
2. Look into the different research opportunities available to you. Pick a few that are interesting

and email the professors stating your interest and qualifications.

3. Put together a spreadsheet listing your goals and all the different opportunities that are available to you right now. Again you will find this template particularly helpful:

Opportunity Template:
(www.internblueprint.com/resources)

4. Research the extra-curricular activities and clubs at your school. Get involved, meet new people, and strive to become a leader. It will pay off greatly in the long term.

Chapter 3 – Marketing Materials

Once you've got some good experience under your belt, it's time to move onto assembling your marketing materials. The number of interviews that you get is directly correlated to how good your materials and how good your materials are being directly correlated to the number of hours you spend refining them. In our experience, almost no one spends enough time getting everything right. We recommend that you set aside a few hours every week dedicated to only working on your marketing materials.

In this section, we will talk about the following:

- Resume
- Cover Letter
- LinkedIn Profile
- Website
- Elevator Pitches

Resume

Your resume is a tailored document that summarizes your work history, educational background, interests and accomplishments and will essentially dictate your career path. If you only intend to put a tiny bit of work into your resume, then you will see little to no reward. It is the most valuable weapon in your internship armory. Understanding its value and knowing how to write an effective resume is instrumental in the job search process.

We understand the entire job application process can be frustrating. Remember, we have been there ourselves. And with each rejection, it can get harder and harder to pull yourself back up. But with some hard work and know-how that you will gain from this course, you can secure that internship. We are 100% sure of it! When you are reading through, make sure to think from a recruiter's point of view. They see hundreds of resumes every single day. How can you stand out?

Throughout this chapter, we will discuss different components of a resume and how to put one together. From there we can then go through the process in detail and apply it to your particular circumstances.

The average college student spends a lot of time working on ensuring they have the highest GPA possible, but then only spends a maximum of a couple of hours putting their resume together. The reality is that resumes are time-consuming to put together and send out. Putting so limited an effort into such an important document is almost like leaving your internship and job prospects to chance.

As we discussed in the earlier chapter, you should be able to add at least one unique point to your resume for each semester that you pay tuition. From a freshman's viewpoint, it stands to reason that you won't have many things to talk about on your resume, apart from high school and possible summer jobs. But do not fret! You have plenty of time to work on it. Remember college is an investment that will help you to build on your resume for each semester you are there.

There are some simple tricks that we will share to make your chances of securing an interview more probable. Once you understand each of the different steps associated with getting and landing your dream internship, learning the mechanics will get you to where you want to go. Anything is possible, however finding the path to get you there is always the challenge.

First, you need to decide how you want to put your resume together. Microsoft Word and LaTeX are the two programs that we would recommend as a superb starting point. To make things as simple as possible, we will include a couple of templates and examples for you to examine at the end of the chapter so you can use them as a baseline in which to create your resume.

The first item you want to include on your resume is your name. Nothing else. Name on the absolute top of your resume. This is because the application tracking systems (ATS), which we will talk more about, specifically looks for a name. This can then be followed by contact information including cell phone number, email, LinkedIn, etc. After you add your information to the top of the resume, then we can work on the following sections;

- Header
- Education
- Experience
- Leadership and Extracurricular Activities
- Publications
- Honors and Awards
- Skills

Header

Many people include much more information in their header than is needed. The only absolutely critical pieces are your name and email. Of course, if you have other things to show off—personal website, Github, or LinkedIn Profile - those should be included as well. If you find yourself in need of another piece of information for aesthetic reasons, you can include your phone number or address.

Github: coderbob
LinkedIn: coderbob

BOB SMITH

http://coderbob.com
bob@coderbob.com

Figure 1: Example of a header section

Education

Since you are still in school, Education should be the first main section of your resume. This can be moved down below experience once you are working.

This section should not be complicated or long. Simply fill in the information about your school and degree in your template of choice.

EDUCATION

B.S., Computer Science	Ball So Hard University	September 2015 – May 2019

• 3.0 GPA. Minor in Mathematics. Concentration in Artificial Intelligence and Data.

Figure 2: example of an education section

You should include your GPA if it is above a 3.0 (or whatever is deemed "good" depending on your school and major). If your in-major GPA is higher than your overall, it is acceptable to substitute it, but make sure to specify that it is not your overall.

If you don't have enough experience in other parts of your resume, you can include a list of relevant classes taken.

Experience

When it comes to your work experience, list it in reverse chronological order from the latest to the earliest. Note the name of the organization and the start and end date of the job. On the second line, write the title and the location of the position, again in city and state format.

Then you can go into more detail about the job using one or two bullet points.

Try to ensure that any experience noted relates to the internship position you are applying for where possible. It may be helpful to keep a list of all of your relevant experiences, so you can look back on it when it comes to customizing your resume for the position. That way you can pick and choose the most relevant ones that highlight your skills.

Rather than merely listing your duties, focus on the actual accomplishments you achieved in the role and quantify the results if you can. Statements which begin with phrases such as "contributed to", "helped to" and "advised on" will all demonstrate your key skills successfully. Keep it short and simple and repeat for each company you have worked with.

We suggest you write in bullet points and not full sentences. Each bullet on your resume should be:

- Impressive
- Focused on results
- Extremely specific

Impressive

The entire point of your resume is to make you stand out in the crowd. If a bullet does not say something impressive about you, it should not be on there! The easiest way to gauge if something is impressive or not is to translate it from resume-speak to plain English and then ask if it is compelling. A phrase commonly seen on resumes is similar to "Completed assigned project under tight deadlines and constraints." What does this mean when you take away the resume-speak? "Did my job." Not so impressive now. One page is not that long, every word needs to earn its way onto the page. If a bullet point could be seen on any random person's resume, it does not belong on yours!

Focused on Results

Description bullets should be focused on the results that you achieved, not on the actions that led to it. What did you build that was not there before? How did that contribute to the goals of your team or organization?

For example, if you had a research position, instead of saying "Carried out various experiments, recorded and analyzed results, and wrote multiple reports," which doesn't actually say much about what value was created, say "Experimentally discovered that x does x, which led to cost savings of 50%.

Extremely Specific

You should always be striving to make your bullets more specific. Add as many details as you can possibly think of. If you can name drop something or someone, do it! Include numbers with your results even if you have to estimate them.

For every one of your bullets, look at it with a critical eye and see if there are any ambiguities with what you've written. If a recruiter is left with any question besides "How did they do so many impressive things?" you still have more work to do.

EXPERIENCE

Data Science Intern	Acme Corporation	May 2017 – August 2017

- Researched deep learning for automated expense reporting from receipt photos taken on Acme's mobile app.
- Designed and trained a custom ResNet for text bounding box detection that achieved over 80% accuracy on real data.
- Developed a training process that achieved over 88% scaling efficiency on 256 GPUs with no loss in accuracy.

Figure 3: Example of experience subsection

Leadership and Extracurricular Activities

At this point in your career, your leadership and extracurricular section may be longer than your experience section. That is no matter. List it the same as you would the work experience category above in reverse chronological order. Consider what you have done to date. Were you the leader of a project or a group? What group activities have you participated in?

Remember, this is where you get the opportunity to expand on your experience. While the skills you list may not be exactly relevant to your internship, these activities will feature your soft skills in a good light. Keep it brief and concise. If you are early on in your college career, you will probably still have space left over on your resume. This is where you will be placing any leadership roles that you have in your extracurriculars.

Sort them in reverse order of impressiveness and make sure to follow all the same rules for writing bullets as the work experience section.

Publications

If you have had the pleasure and the fortune of contributing to a paper, then this is the place to write it down. List all contributors as noted on the text or in the publication, followed by the title of the work and the publishing house it was published by. If it was for a magazine or other periodical, then note the date instead of the publishing house.

PUBLICATIONS

- Parker, Ray (Rensselaer Polytechnic Institute). "Regolith and Environment Science & Oxygen and Lunar Volatile Extraction (RESOLVE) Project." National Aeronautics and Space Administration, KSC, August 2013.
- Chollangi, Srinivas, Ray Parker, and Yi Li. "Development of Robust Antibody Purification by Optimizing Protein-A Chromatography in Combination with Precipitation Methodologies." Biotechnology & Bioengineering. Wiley.

Figure 4: Example of a publications section

Honors and Awards

Hopefully, you will have received an honor or award to add to this list. Write them all in one sentence, interspersed by commas to differentiate between each one. If you don't have any to date, then leave the section out altogether. You can proudly add this section back in when you do finally receive an award or acknowledgment. Never, ever feel the need to embellish if you don't have them.

- 1st Place, 2016 Sponsor Buzzword Hackathon
- 2nd Place, 2017 BSH Entrepreneurship Award
- 3rd Place, 2017 Midwest Trading Competition
- Finalist, 2017 State Business Competition
- Honoree, 2015-2016 BSH Dean's List
- Honoree, 2015 BSHHS Scholarship

Figure 5: Example of an awards section

Skills

The skills that you list will depend on the position you are applying to. More than anything, this section is for adding keywords to your resume that you might not have gotten in otherwise. Start by writing down the languages and frameworks that you know best and work with the most. When you are applying to each position, you can add in the skills that they ask for in the job description. Even if you don't know the skill amazingly well, it is fine to put it on there as long as you can brush up on it in time for an interview.

For each section of your resume, make sure you refer back to our resume example and template for proper formatting.

SKILLS

- **Data Science:** Python (MXNet, scikit-learn, SciPy), Java + Scala (Apache Spark, Storm), Lua (Torch)
- **Data Visualization:** Python (ggplot, seaborn, matplotlib), Javascript (D3.js)
- **Natural Language Processing:** Python (spaCy, gensim, NLTK)
- **Application Development:** Python, Java, Scala (Akka), C++, C
- **Other:** LaTeX, Git, Unix, SQL, NoSQL (MongoDB, DynamoDB)

Figure 6: Example of a skills section

We recommend getting your resume critiqued by multiple people who you think have it figured out. There will always be things that you missed, whether it is spelling and grammar or a bullet point that you can be more specific on. Work with one person at a time until you get their approval, then move onto the next. If two people disagree on something, go to the third. More than three is usually excessive.

But if you think that your resume is good and you don't need others to look at it, remember that this document will single-handedly determine how many interviews you get.

Remember that as a freshman, you won't have as many different types of experiences, knowledge or skills. By joining clubs and getting into research projects, you can get a running start on many of your peers. While listing everything you have done to date on your CV will fill up the paper, it won't necessarily highlight your best assets. You need to have a basic framework for how to choose what to put on your resume. Don't be afraid to prioritize certain internships over others, especially if they are with a high-profile company. While you may have part-time positions or summer jobs you want to include, these can be dropped off in favor of other more notable internships when you get more experience. The same goes for your extracurricular activities. The more experiences and projects you work on, the pickier you can become of what you put on your resume and what you leave off of it. Keep that in mind.

Keep it brief and coherent, exceeding no more than two pages in length. Bullet points will come in handy and can be used to list your accomplishments. It also allows you to add a lot of information in a short space. Always try to tailor your resume for the job description you have in mind, and refer back to our resume examples and templates when in doubt.

Out in the job hunting jungle, there are programs called automated Application Tracking Systems (ATS) that automatically parse your resume to see how much of a match you are for a particular position. Literally, every single application that you submit online (unless it is sent by email) will go through an applicant tracking system these days. This is very relevant to your applications and comes back to how much attention you paid to the job description. These automated systems are set to look for keywords and specific phrases, such as types of software, company names, and skills. To get past the robot and even get your resume in front of a recruiter, you have two strategies: beat the robot or skip it altogether.

Application Tracking Systems

The robot or the ATS is challenging to get past, we won't sugarcoat it! But, making sure you have enough of the same keywords as the job listing will help to increase your chances of success tremendously! Remember, the hirer wants to see a demonstrated awareness of all the skills they mention and more. Stick to the following layout, and you can't go wrong!

For robotic purposes, the very first line of your resume should have your first and last name. Nothing else!

Next, you should list your contact information including your email, phone number, LinkedIn URL, personal website and any other details relevant here. It's often unnecessary to put in your home address because it isn't essential for the position unless it's a strategic advantage to tell them where you are located.

Try to refrain from adding a professional summary or block of text which talks about yourself. This is not necessary when it comes to engineering/science internships, and it can work against you by limiting the number of opportunities you are considered for.

For example, if you are a chemical engineer looking for process design experience in the pharmaceutical industry, you might think it wise to add a summary statement such as, *"Currently looking for a process design summer internship in the pharmaceutical industry to gain exposure and explore career opportunities."*

However, if a recruiter was looking to fill a summer internship position in a manufacturing setting, that could cause them to overlook you for that particular opportunity.

Granted, if you are customizing your resume for each job, then this should not be an obstacle. However, in certain circumstances (which we will cover later), there are a couple of opportunities where you won't be able to tailor for every single position, resulting in a more generalized resume. Chances are, if they truly want to see how well you write, they will ask to see a sample of your writing.

Customization

The most common question we hear when it comes to customizing your resume is:

"Do I have to customize my resume for every SINGLE position I apply for?"

Our answer is always: *"Yes, up until a certain point."*

Customizing your resume will take time. But the great news is that once you submit enough applications and customize enough resumes and cover letters, there will be a certain workflow you will accomplish that will streamline the process. You can use shortcuts such as Ctrl+F in Word to find and replace company names, job titles, etc. Your shortcuts will become your standard, and you will soon find ways to speed up the process.

Whenever you put together a resume or cover letter, there will always be a customized paragraph you need to add. Unfortunately, there is no such thing as one-resume-fits-all positions, so try and customize for each industry and position up to a certain point.

Remember, recruiters are looking for keywords so make sure you are using relevant keywords and subjects applicable to the job and the company. It will solidify your interest in the position and show your potential to succeed.

Do, however, always make sure you proofread each customized application. There is nothing worse than sending an application with the wrong company or person's name on it, and it may just be put straight into the reject pile without a second thought. The minute or two you spend proofreading is ALWAYS worth it.

Length of your Resume

The chances are that when you walk into the career center at your university and show them your resume, the first thing they will tell you is that your resume should be one page - maximum. For specific applications that is perfectly fine, such as when you are submitting it at a career fair. But, for online applications, you may find it is just not long enough. It is vital that you feather your resume with lots of relevant keywords and text to pass the applicant tracking systems and be seen by the recruiters. That can be particularly difficult to do when you are trying to keep it below the maximum length of one page.

When you are submitting your resume in person, maintain your focus on your elevator pitch, and keep your resume condensed so as not to overwhelm the recruiter. For example, a more seasoned intern may have five or six internship positions and that can be difficult to highlight all on one page and attract the attention of the recruiters. Give yourself as much space as necessary without going overboard. A sophomore in college or a freshman will only require one page until they have some more experience up their sleeve.

Having a robust work experience section will attract a lot more viewers to your profile. Outline each point and add as much as detail as you can. What software have you used? How many projects have you worked on? What was their main focus? If you have any quantitative improvement metrics, you can include those in as well. Be as descriptive as possible and make sure to write in the third person.

When it comes to detailing your experience on LinkedIn, your descriptions will have more detail, but overall the idea is the same.

Here are some links to some useful templates and helpful examples which you can use to your advantage.

Resume Example & Resume Template:
(www.internblueprint.com/resources)

Cover Letter

So, let's get back to basics for a moment.

What exactly is a cover letter?

A cover letter is a supplement to your resume which allows you to elaborate in more detail about certain areas which are relevant to the position. They help you to send information to recruiters and companies, so they can get an entire picture of your background and experience. You can add additional information that isn't covered on the resume and highlight specific points of interest that may only apply to this one position. Your cover letter should answer the question "why should we interview you for this job?" Too many people make the mistake of simply restating what is on their resume in prose. Remember that it is a supplement for your resume, not a replacement. Besides, they provide you with an opportunity to use those keywords and phrases and detail your skills and software to give your resume a better chance of passing the robots and being seen by the recruiter.

A cover letter is a one-page document that allows you to state your goal and purpose of writing the letter, in your case, to secure a possible employment or internship opportunity. It gets sent in with your resume and should ALWAYS be customized towards the particular company or industry. It will tend to be around four paragraphs in length.

Paragraph 1:

This initial section will cover why you want to work for that one particular company. It will be tailored to a certain industry and will consist of much-customized information which is specific to the organization you are addressing.

Paragraph 2:

Next, elaborate on specific points about yourself and advise them on how you can add value to the company and solve their problems efficiently. Also, try to outline your soft skills which are listed in the specific job description and tailor your resume to show how you can demonstrate those skills. If you're able to customize this paragraph for each position, you apply for without cutting any corners, it will allow you to be more in-depth and more focused than the majority of the other applicants.

Paragraph 3:

The third paragraph should talk about some of the other concerns. If there are issues such as gaps in between employment or a very low GPA, then you can specifically mention these in your cover lever. Provide information that isn't covered on the resume that you would like to include, or things that will help you stand out from all the other applicants.

Paragraph 4:

The final paragraph should talk about an ask. By an ask, we mean something actionable or something you are looking for. It is pertinent to include your contact information. One more interesting, yet optional, thing to do is to ask for some type of task or assignment at the end of the cover letter. Perhaps something along the lines of:

"If you wish to see my work abilities in action, feel free to send me an assignment to gauge my performance."

A comment such as this will allow you to gain more traction and even spur the recruiter or hiring manager to action.

As far as the order goes, try to stick to this layout as much as possible to inadvertently avoid leaving relevant details out. It will help during the customization stage if all of your letters are roughly the same format.

Cover letters are essential in mainstream recruitment although, customarily, you may find that you are applying in person or online, sending in resumes through referrals, or cold emailing recruiters. If that is the case, then tech position applications don't require an extensive cover letter. It still pays to add one where you can, although they won't be as necessary in some cases.

So, if you do want to create a cover letter that will get you noticed, make sure to utilize the template that we've included. Be confident and enthusiastic, and use specific language relevant to the position when talking about your accomplishments. Don't rehash what's on your resume but to try to come at it from a new angle. The cover letter is your chance to show why you are uniquely qualified for the job outside of the facts already stated on your resume.

Use these templates to your advantage, as you did before with the resume section and make sure to look at some of the examples as well.

Here's an example of a cover letter that was created following this process:

"Dear Hiring Manager,

I am extremely excited to be able to apply for a software engineering internship at Airbnb. Here are two reasons why I am a perfect fit for this role.

First, I am passionate about hospitality. My parents have been proud Airbnb hosts almost since the platform's inception. I have always loved the variety of people that we have met while hosting! We would always try to make sure that we gave them the absolute best experience possible. I strongly believe in your mission and would be honored to be a part of furthering it.

Second, I have extensive experience in software engineering. Last summer, I interned at Acme, a leading startup for widgets, where I designed, developed, and put into production a feature that made more widgets. By fooing the bar, I was able to increase our widget output by 15% while reducing cost by 5%. Along the way, we ran into problems x and y, but were able to mitigate their consequences by baring the foo.

I'm confident that my skills and experience would be a great asset to Airbnb and I'd love to chat with you about the role in greater detail.

Sincerely,
Bob Smith"

Cover Letter Example & Cover Letter Template:
(www.internblueprint.com/resources)

LinkedIn

LinkedIn profiles can positively impact the way working professionals look at you, even before you begin your working career.

LinkedIn will act as your "digital resume" as well as aid in your networking efforts later on. A common practice after meeting someone professionally in real life is to connect with them on LinkedIn so that you can stay in touch. You will be able to see who they are connected with and vice-versa. When it comes time to find people who work for your target companies, having many LinkedIn connections will be immensely valuable.

Make sure to personalize your LinkedIn URL and put it on your resume as well as your email signature. That can result in a lot of potential leads and help inform you as to who is looking at your LinkedIn profile. Adding multimedia can help make your LinkedIn sparkle.

Ultimately, the wider you spread your net to make connections and join groups, the larger your affiliations will be. This will help narrow down the degrees of connection which can be helpful in getting your name out in the industry. The more people you befriend on the social networking site, the better.

If you don't have an account yet, we strongly recommend that you create on as soon as possible. In this section, we will discuss the major elements of a great profile:

- Profile Picture
- Headline
- Summary
- Work Experience
- Recommendations

Profile Picture

Your LinkedIn photo needs to be a professional headshot of you in a formal setting or something that relates to your field of interest. Avoid any picture of you looking unprofessional at all measures. Here are some useful guidelines to make you seem more approachable.

- Make sure your face is shown completely.
- Choose a photo that looks like you.
- Dress in corporate attire.
- And don't forget to smile.

Headline

The next thing most people will look at after the picture is the 120-character description. LinkedIn will automatically populate your headline for you, which means that you need to customize it to your benefit! If viewed on a mobile device, note that only the first 90-odd characters will be visible so make those count! The main point we want to make here is that you need to be memorable, yet professional, so recruiters will want to learn more about you.

There is no right or wrong way, but anything you write will be more captivating than LinkedIn's standard "Student at Rensselaer Polytechnic Institute", or "Mechanical Engineering Student at Carnegie Mellon."

Here are some examples of headlines that work well:

- Information Based: "Chemical Engineer, experience in venture capital, consulting, pharma and aerospace. Seeking full-time employment for the summer of 2017."

- Keyword Based: "Data Scientist | SQL | Machine Learning | Full Stack Web Dev | Computer Science Student"

- Achievement Based: "CEO at _____ | 3,000+ Connections | Helping Business Growth | Appointing Opportunities | Building Success | Open Networker"

Summary

Your summary is your online elevator pitch that will give the recruiter a clear overview of your professional career, education, qualifications you have, and a bit about your personality. While it will not be the first or even the second thing that catches a recruiter's eye, they will get around to reading it eventually to see if you are a comfortable fit for the culture of their organization. They will use your personalized summary to get a better understanding of you and your professional background. Here are some guidelines for writing your own.

- Keep it short
- Add pertinent keywords
- Include a specific value proposition

LinkedIn is all about selling yourself and your services. Being able to market yourself extensively is what will set you apart from the rest of your peers. Whenever you sit down to write your summary, be sure to include your skills and core strengths that you wish to highlight to the recruiters who might be reading your profile. Your summary is one of the few places where you can expand on your talents and tell a story that will help differentiate you from others.

Your summary should include:

- Extended elevator pitch or story which should be told in the first person
- Specific content focusing on accomplishments
- Your mission
- Individual strengths
- URL to personal website
- Necessary contact information

Work Experience

Prospective recruiters will look at your work experience and keywords to find matches to the positions they are looking to recruit for. Also, having a robust work experience section helps attract a lot more viewers to your profile. Outline each point carefully and add lots of details about the type of software you used, how many projects you worked on. Finish with quantitative improvement metrics if you have them. Be as descriptive as possible and always write in the third person.

In the world of LinkedIn, having more profile views puts you at the top of the search algorithm, which can lead to more interviews and potential opportunities in the future. A professional profile will attract the recruiters and interest the employers.

As a student, you may not have a lot of work experience up your sleeve. To avoid a blank resume, highlight any involvement with the community during your university years. This may include volunteering for causes, participating in events, certifications, courses, awards – anything you can think of that will enhance your experience.

For each entry, include a robust description of your roles & responsibilities and key achievements throughout the term. For example, *"Worked at a coffee shop"* can be easily rewritten as:

"Worked part-time at Starbucks Coffee as a barista. Interacted with 50+ customers each day and reported sales to the manager each month. Consistently performed reliable customer service every week."

See the difference?

When putting down your work experience, be sure to use relevant keywords and enhanced job descriptions. Don't leave anything out. It doesn't have to be as condensed as a resume. Therefore, make sure your duties are descriptive enough to give whoever is reading it, a well-rounded view of what your day-to-day tasks might look like.

We have added a link below which provides excellent examples of LinkedIn profiles and descriptions. Use this to your advantage.

Recommendations

Not having any recommendations won't hurt your profile too much, but having an extremely good one will give it extra credibility. We recommend that you first trade recommendations with the people that you have worked with in the past, whether formally in a job or class project or informally on a personal project.

Next, if you've had a job or research position in the past, you should approach your former superior and nicely ask them if they could write a short recommendation. Since you already have other recommendations on your profile from your peers, they have something to go off of and are much more likely to agree. It also helps to offer to write a recommendation for their profile, though in our experience they always decline.

All other sections available on LinkedIn — skills, education, classes, and a few more — can be copied from your resume directly.

If you are new to LinkedIn, you should import your contacts and connect with everyone on that list. This will bootstrap your network on the platform and give you a considerable boost in the search rankings as well as allow more people that you know in real life to find you.

Finally, you should change the default URL, which will frequently be something like "bob-smith-17469". This is hard to read, say, and link to and should be changed to something closer to "rayparker" or "ray-parker".

LinkedIn Profile Examples:
(www.internblueprint.com/resources)

Personal Website

The next piece of marketing material that you must create is a personal website. This is mainly because it's one of those things that almost no one has and it's a smart way to stand out against everybody else and launch your professional career. Think of yourself as a brand that you want to market as far and as wide as possible.

If a prospective employer receives your resume and believes you are a worthy candidate for the role, chances are they are going to search your name. A personal website allows you to control the content they see and will ensure that your name comes up in an internet search. Most people in your age will only have social media pages, Facebook and Twitter perhaps. You automatically become a more attractive candidate because you have taken the time to create your own website.

A website demonstrates to hirers that you are tech savvy, can develop your own website and publish it on the internet. It proves you are technologically competent regardless of how basic the site is.

It also makes you more visible, allowing you to add your website link everywhere. Any time you email a recruiter or a professor, note your link at the bottom. Put it on your resume and list it on your LinkedIn profile, so everything links back to your website. That way you can have all of your information organized in one single place and showcase your projects and research to your advantage.

Make sure your homepage acts as a central landing page where you can convey the essence of what you're about. The homepage can either include a couple of short, catchy bullet points or a paragraph of introduction. From here, you can link to the About page which is where you can have your resume laid out in full. Like LinkedIn, you can add more details than you would find on your regular resume as you are not limited by page numbers.

Fill it out with as much detail as you possibly can. If you have experience in a number of industries, then you can add additional pages or more content, but for the moment, feel free to keep it as simple as possible while you get started. You can add miscellaneous pages as you go – whatever you think will give a well-rounded view of the person you are. You can list the latest books you are reading, add your favorite quotes, sprinkle in a few photos, link to your LinkedIn profile, create a portfolio, write a blog - whatever you think your readers may find valuable. It is these pages which will ensure you stand out from other student websites which are basically just an online resume. You don't necessarily need to include any special pages, but having them will differentiate you from the others.

Here is a list of different sections to have on your personal website. Each of these are flexible and can be molded to what you want to convey.

- **Home:** Talk a bit about yourself and summarize each of the sections you cover in your website.
- **About:** Biography on yourself, what you do for fun, what you are interested in and future plans.
- **Work:** Usually a repository of all your work experience, including links and descriptions.
- **Links:** Github, LinkedIn, email, Social Media, and PDF copies of your resume can be put here.
- **Consulting:** If you'd like to offer your expertise, list of services you offer and how you can help.
- **Blog:** Scratchpad for all your different ideas and thoughts that you'd like to share with individuals who come to your website. Keep it professional.
- **Contact:** List of ways for individuals to keep in contact with you, from social media to email.

If you are a computer science major, then you should make an effort to try and code your website yourself. You can base it off a template and make changes to customize the navigation and style. PHP is not that hard to learn if you're a computer science major and it is very easy to set yourself up with WordPress. If you are not interested in designing your own, then you can use a simple template from Weebly, Squarespace, or whatever website maker out there. You may have to pay a small amount of money to get started, but again it is an investment rather than an expense. When someone types your name into Google, that's the first thing you want to pop up.

Whichever route you decide to go down, don't forget to update your website regularly. And always, always keep it professional. Write it as if your grandmother were reading it!

In summary, keep it relevant and up to date.

Below are some well-honed examples of personal websites that may inspire your passion and creativity.

- rayokadaparker.com
- charlieyou.me
- jwdunne.com
- devonbernard.com

Elevator Pitch

Can you guess what the number one thing is that recruiters look for at a career fair? It is not your experience or your background. In actual fact, it is your ability to talk and communicate that will draw their attention. This is the main reason why career fairs are done in such an open-ended formal setting. It gives potential hirers an advantage as they can see how well you interact with others in a reasonably professional environment.

Now, what do you think is the most asked question at interviews? It's always the dreaded *"tell me about yourself"* question. This is the very first question a recruiter will ask you, and it is critical that you have your elevator pitch ready. Your answer will subsequently set the tone for the rest of the interview.

The elevator pitch is the first thing you should prepare when you are planning to attend a career fair, followed by your resume and cover letter. There are a couple of different ways to do this and some very specific things you should consider.

First, talk about yourself, your background and what your interests are. From there, you can delve into your knowledge of the company, what you like about them and what you would like to do at the company. Discussing how you can add specific value should be high on your priority list as it is a direct reflection of your worth and is applicable both in an interview and in a career setting.

Here is a suitable example which you can amend to fit your particular circumstances.

"Hi, I'm Ray Parker, a chemical engineering Senior at RPI. I help customers of large, innovative companies find the best solutions for their needs. Last summer, I interned at Booz Allen Hamilton where I consulted with the EPA to develop corrosion sensors which detected the amount of lead in drinking water with 80% accuracy."

Just like the resume bullet descriptions, you should only include the highlights of your career and be extremely specific about the results that you achieved.

The second part of your pitch will be more focused on the company and role you are applying to. State your interest in the role and how you can help their company meet its goals.

"I am extremely interested in a consulting internship with Salesforce. Given my past experience in similar roles, I am confident that I can help your customers fulfill their needs with products within the Salesforce ecosystem. I'd love to answer any questions you have about my background or how I can help Salesforce."

Just like with your resume, if you are applying to companies in different industries, you should customize which past experiences you highlight.

Be prepared to articulate certain specifics rather than make generic references. Direct conversation will ensure you get a position similar to what you want to do rather than what they may think you want to do. Don't be afraid to discuss your long-term goals and where your ambitions lie. Having the main body of your elevator pitch prepared in advance will allow you to be more communicative at the fair. It will also go a long way to positioning your skills in a professional light, regardless of your experience.

We recommend that you practice saying it out loud enough times that you can do it smoothly under duress. Fire up a voice recorder on your phone and record yourself saying it until every "um" and "uh" are eliminated. This will be a painful process since many don't like the sound of their own voice, but the payoff will be worth it when you find yourself able to deliver it without thinking.

To simplify things, we have included a couple of different links below to each of the different sections of the elevator pitch: How to set one up, how to practice it well and how to make sure that you'll be able to secure your interviews and the next phone call and get the internship that you want.

We have provided a straightforward template at the end of the chapter that you can use if you are unsure of how you can add value to a company, particularly if you're a freshman or sophomore, or you're still undecided about which career path to take. Begin by introducing yourself. Tell them your name, your major, whether you're a junior, senior, sophomore, and what school you go to. Follow it up with your concentration and minor and then list your accomplishments that are relevant to the company in order of impressiveness. Finish up by saying that you are looking for an internship for the summer (or whatever date you have in mind.)

Start with something like this: *"I'm Charlie, a computer science junior at RPI studying data and AI, minoring in math"*. Then list your valid accomplishments and close with the fact that you are looking for a co-op or internship.

From there you can either hand them your resume if it's an interview, or if it's a career fair, then they may look through things or ask you more questions. They may ask you to explain a few things on your resume in more detail, especially if you have a project with an eye-catching name. Hopefully, by this stage, you are well practiced in your interview techniques and have prepared answers just perfect for such an occasion. The delivery of your pitch should be a higher priority than the content. And the only way to perfect the delivery is to practice, practice and practice some more.

If you are committed to landing an internship and are seeking to achieve perfection, then it will pay to download a voice recording app on your computer and repeat your elevator pitch over and over again in a variety of settings. Everything should be timed and memorized perfectly to avoid nervous pauses and the um's and ah's which can often accompany unprepared speeches. So, even if there is a major distraction, like someone trying to talk to you while you are giving your elevator pitch or a tornado going through your town while you happen to be applying for a job, you should be able to deliver your pitch perfectly. Hopefully, that latter situation will never occur, however.

We believe you will find the links to this chapter particularly helpful and wish you best of luck with your practice.

Elevator Pitch Template:
(www.internblueprint.com/resources)

It is here where your efforts should be starting to come together. You should be satisfied with how you are spending your time and have begun to see real progress in your website, resume and elevator pitch.

Once you have your materials ready, you can then move on to scouring the internet and newspapers and finding suitable internships. All the work you have done up until this point will enable you to be better placed to land you an interview. Never underestimate the preliminary research and preparation. So don't skimp on your efforts. Your resume, cover letter, and website may be the only things they see of you, so make those first impressions count. Apply these to your applications and turn them into interviews, and ideally into offers.

Chapter FAQs and Action Items

How much time should I spend on putting my resume together?

The answer: a lot. The average college student only spends around two hours on writing out, formatting and proofreading their resume. That is just not enough to do the job properly. Unfortunately, we recommend spending at least five hours on it to ensure it reads well, is error-free and will get past the computers that will be guarding those opportunities. You NEED to put in that much time, and more, to get the Return On Investment (ROI) that you will need to be successful.

What are the biggest mistakes in cover letters?

The three top mistakes we see when it comes to cover letters are as follows:

- Restating what has already been said on their resume: There is no need. Try to make it an original document to support your resume, not replicate it.

- Failure to give an ask: Be clear on what you want. Demonstrate your willingness by going the extra step.

- Not writing a cover letter at all: This is an error that many students seeking an internship make. They underestimate its value and lose yet another opportunity to stand out.

Also, make sure you do your resume and cover letter together to ensure you are maximizing your application chances.

Action Items – 10+ Hours

Now that you know what an internship is and have the necessary experience to lay the groundwork for yourself, it's time to put your knowledge into practice. By utilizing our techniques and strategies you will have a handful of solid materials that will be vital in establishing your career.

As we said in the beginning of this chapter, almost no one spends enough time getting these things right. Remember, the better your marketing materials are, the more interviews you'll get. Now for the action steps:

1. Look over your resume with a critical eye and find areas where you need to make changes. We find that after reading this chapter, some students need to replace over 50% of their existing resume!

Resume Example & Resume Template, Cover Letter Example & Cover Letter Template:
(www.internblueprint.com/resources)

2. Go through and extrapolate your resume and cover letter into a personal website and LinkedIn profile. Remember, LinkedIn or your website will not be customized for a particular job, but your resume and cover letter will need to be!

    LinkedIn Profile Example:
    (www.internblueprint.com/resources)

3. Ask three people to critique your resume. Make the edits they suggest. After you have an acceptable version, proceed with the next steps, but continue to periodically review and edit it. There will always be something you can improve.

4. Craft your elevator pitch, customize it and practice it often.

5. Write the first draft of the cover letter template for the industry the majority of your applications are going to. Have a friend look at this as well and make edits. Use this to write a cover email for each industry as well.

6. Setup a LinkedIn page or edit your existing one and customize the URL.

7. Register your name's domain name and create a personal website. An ultra-barebones one is

good enough for now, but you should plan on eventually expanding it.

Elevator Pitch Template:
(www.internblueprint.com/resources)

Chapter 4 – Finding Internships

After you have your marketing materials in order, the next step is to make a list of everywhere that you plan on applying. Many of you will want to apply to each internship as you find them, but we believe this is a mistake. First, it will be much more efficient if you separate the two tasks and second, it allows you to be much more strategic. For example, if you are in the enviable position of having lots of good experience, you can apply to the companies you would most like to work for first so that you don't end up sending out frivolous applications.

We suggest that you add each position you find to a spreadsheet for easier tracking. We have a template for this available in the resources section on our website.

(www.internblueprint.com/resources)

Some companies receive upwards of 10,000 applications for only 10 positions. That is quite a scary prospect, right? When you look at it from that perspective, it is clear that to maximize your chances, you need to be seen in as many places as possible and optimize your strategy to make up for the competitive job market. Think of it as a numbers game, but it doesn't always have to be because there are steps you can take to make yourself a better candidate. The more you send out, the higher your success rate, but always prioritize quality over quantity.

There are multiple ways of finding out about the internships available to you. In this chapter, we will discuss:

- Your school's resources
- How to network to find opportunities
- Useful online resources such as job boards and corporate websites.

Then, we will top it off with FAQs and practical action steps necessary to be successful.

School Resources

Job Boards

Each school will have an individual online job board; that fact is pretty simple for anyone to get their head around. However, depending on the quality of the school, some will be better than others! It enables you to go online and submit your resume for potential recruiters to view. It (like many other university websites) is an excellent tool to have up your sleeve. It publishes a wide variety of job postings from entry level positions through to jobs for alumni with ten plus years of experience in their field. It even advertises a range of volunteer posts. JobLink is a brilliant starting point, and it is indeed worthwhile spending your time to fill out your profile and keep it current with projects and experience. Check out the offerings that your school has, or if you are unsure, ask your career center advisor.

Handshake (www.joinhandshake.com) is another prominent website accessed by over 8,000,000 students, 400 universities and 200,000 employers (and counting). Make a note of it and see what opportunities you can find. Websites and apps like this are ultimately the way of the future. Therefore, surf the sites and use them as a font of knowledge on all thing internship related.

Sites such as JobLink and Handshake tend to allow you to add a personalized profile, very similar to LinkedIn. Here you can list any internship experience you have had or failing that, any research projects or relevant groups that you have been involved in. Be as descriptive as you can with your details as that will motivate individuals or companies to recruit you directly from the school site. Use it as an avenue to get your name out there, but don't even depend on any particular resource too heavily as it may not become fruitful.

Once your resume, cover letter, LinkedIn profile and personal website are up to date and have been checked for errors, we recommend that you go through all the job sites and try to filter out and apply for positions that you are interested in. If you go to a prominent tech university such as RPI, it can help you broaden your scope and skill set focus. On the same note, there are a lot of liberal arts schools, state schools and other educational supported websites which are just as popular and offer equally valuable resources. One of the particular advantages about JobLink is that it allows you to see how many other individuals you're in competition with. If you scroll down to a local university level, there is always going to be much less competition for a position. Once you get applying to jobs on a national or international level then the stakes change and you're going to be competing with a lot of other students from different schools.

School resource-based websites such as JobLink are beneficial when it comes to sourcing internships as well as jobs. Even reputable companies such as Bristol-Myers Squibb, SpaceX and others, search for suitable intern applicants using these sites. They won't hesitate to reach out to individual candidates if they believe that someone is qualified to work with them. Truthfully, you never know what companies may be looking at your online profile, so it pays to have all your details up to date and polished. There could be someone looking at it right now! Think on it for a moment. If that is the case and someone is looking at it today, would they want to hire you on the basis of your current profile? Do you think you can make further changes to improve it? Can you reword it so you come across as more qualified or could you showcase your experience in a better light?

The College Career Professional Development (CCPD) is another resource we have on Rensselaer's campus. You can always go and talk to your career center about your resume, cover letter, career advice or salary negotiations; whenever you need. However, from our experience, they aren't always as helpful as they could be. In fact, only 52% of US college graduates actually go to the career center once in their undergraduate years. If you do use it, bear in mind, it may not be as useful as you may have initially hoped. Saying that, they can be useful for basic tasks such as spell checking and proofreading. But if you want more career-specific advice, then forget it! It is a shame really as their hearts are in the right place and the staff that work in the career centers are routinely keen to assist. Colleges and career centers need to seriously rethink how they can better support the students in this primarily tech-focused age.

Take it from us, do your homework, follow our suggestions, and you will have a much better success rate when it comes to applying for tech-specific internships and visiting career fairs.

Career Fairs

As we mentioned before, career fairs are an excellent way to find internship opportunities. One of the most valuable things you can do with your time is to attend them. Honestly, that's one of the things we love most about RPI, and we presume the same applies to other university career fairs across the country. The connections you make at a career fair are invaluable. Most of the time, companies will send alumni to these sorts of events, and having that university connection may go far; you never know. Getting those interviews will go a long way to making that tuition and those fees seem like they are worth it, especially if you can get a life-changing internship from it.

Check to see whether your university offers any specialized career fairs which may work to your advantage. Your university may also provide community service career fairs for unpaid internships or other things of that nature. Landing one of those is a noteworthy first step on the career ladder. Positions like these will help you pad out your resume and give you something to add to your personal website, cover letter and more. Definitely exhaust every opportunity you can on campus, because you never know where it may lead!

Networking

Networking should be high on your priority list when it comes to recruitment and searching for an internship. And thankfully, regardless of how sociable you are, there are many different ways to network.

Information Sessions

Information sessions are talks given by recruiters and employees that provide a little bit of information about the company, what they do, and who they are looking to hire. These are fantastic opportunities to get a better sense of what a company is like and to meet some of the employees. You should try to attend every information session you can, even if you are on the fence about a certain company. You might find that a company is not what you originally thought and want to work for them after all. Best of all, not that many students will go to these and so it is a great way to stand out to the recruiters there.

You would be surprised at the number of students who don't turn up to events such as this. What a waste of an opportunity. Go and talk to each one of the different recruiters. Bring your resume along, dress professionally (if appropriate) and speak to each individual about their company.

Unless you find out you don't want to work for that company, you should talk to every employee there. Give them a little bit about your background and ask if you could potentially be a good fit. Also ask any questions about the company that you have. If you don't have any, here are some that are frequently helpful:

- Why did you decide to join the company?
- What do you think the company could improve at?
- Is there anything you wish someone had told you before you joined?

After all your questions have been answered, thank them and ask if you can contact them if you have any more questions. Most will say yes and give you their business card or email address. The next day, send them a short email thanking them again. This is absolutely crucial and almost no one does it! You make an immediate good first impression and now have contacts within the company to get a referral from when you apply.

Extracurricular Activities

This is another networking method which many students fail to realize. Regardless of the fraternity you are a member of, there will always be a number of different fraternity/sorority networking sessions, alumni weekends, and LinkedIn alumni networking events that you can attend. Get your name out there, let other fraternity/sorority members know your career goals, and talk to as many people as possible. It just makes sense!

Your fraternity/sorority ties can help you secure internships and is often an untapped resource by many students. Consider this: Alumni will be more willing to assist you to find work than a complete stranger.

You have something in common with them for starters and it makes for an easy introduction to the discussion. Just remember to be genuinely interested in what they have to say. Try to avoid putting the focus back to you, even though furthering your career goals is the ultimate reason for chatting with them. Cultivate your conversations and relationships. Your alumni can help you in situations you never even thought possible.

Always keep that adage in the forefront of your mind - it's not what you know, but who you know! You get the picture!

Cold Emailing

At this stage of the internship search, anything is worth a try. Cold emailing individuals who might be interested in what you offer may sound like a long shot, but the reality is you never know what they are looking for at any given time. If they cannot help you, perhaps they know someone who can.

Reaching out and establishing a connection with another individual is a wonderful way to start forming networks. And if you approach it the right way, you will be remembered. At the beginning of the process, your contacts are going to be naturally limited. Cold emailing is a wonderful way to grow those connections. Each email you send out will give you more practice in this area. The trick is to understand what you want from the email. Have a clear ask in mind with a definitive call to action.

Attend Events

Going to conferences, dinner celebrations, actually any event that provides an opportunity to chat with like-minded people, should be a high priority. Just do it! Choose events over parties as it will bring better results and give you plenty of opportunities to talk to individuals and grow your social circle. Active networking will be the key to your success.

You want to be in a position where you can show them what you can do and how you can add value to their organization. It all comes down to that elevator pitch – so rehearse it until you can do it in your sleep. While networking can occur anywhere, even in the most unconventional of situations, going out of your way to source effective networking connections will ensure you are well-prepared.

We will cover more techniques and opportunities to network efficiently later on in the book. Practice and use what you have learned so far.

Online Resources

The internet is by far the easiest way to find a large amount of internships quickly. The downside is that you don't have the advantage of the company actively recruiting from your school or knowing anyone who works there. However, it is an indispensable resource especially if you go to a less-than-stellar school which won't have many of the opportunities we have previously talked about.

There are three main places that you can source internships online:

- Company Websites

- Job Aggregation Sites
- Job Boards

Company Websites

List every single tech company that you can think of and go to their website. If you are interested and they're hiring (they probably are), go to their jobs page (sometimes labeled as "careers") and check if they have internship openings. If they have them, add it to your spreadsheet. If it is not listed, it is possible that they haven't put them up yet. Run an internet search for "[company name] internship" and see if anything comes up. Even if it does not, you can cold email a recruiter (see the next chapter) to know for sure if they offer internships.

Job Aggregation Sites

Job aggregations sites are websites put together by a third party that list companies and open positions. One that we recommend is Intern Supply (www.intern.supply). It lists many different companies with open internships that you can then research and add to your spreadsheet.

Another helpful place to look, especially if you are applying to startups, is venture capital websites. Click through to their portfolio companies and see which ones are interesting to you. AngelList is another fantastic website to go to find positions at startups (www.angel.co/jobs).

Job Boards

Finally, there are job boards. Not all are created equal, and four we recommend in particular is Glassdoor, LinkedIn, Internships and Indeed. Browse through each one to get a feel for their navigation and information.

Glassdoor

One of the major upsides to Glassdoor's website (www.glassdoor.com) is that it has a considerable sized job board where companies will post details of their current internships. Many of the big corporates will post their jobs on there so check in regularly. Do keep an eye out for duplicates however to avoid applying more than once for the same position. Some startups will advertise their internships on there as well.

Two of the benefits of Glassdoor's website is the fact that it features rankings and pay details, so you can quickly filter out companies that have less than four stars or pay below a specific salary. This useful feature can cut hours off your surfing and research time. Pay particular attention to the Interviews tab as this is where interviewees can add past interview questions onto the website. This crowdsourcing of interview questions offers a varied perspective on a wide range of positions. Be sure to check it out before your interviews!

LinkedIn

LinkedIn (www.linkedin.com/jobs) is the job board that everyone who's anyone uses. It is the place to be if you are seeking an internship. Truthfully, however, if you are serious about your career then you must set up your LinkedIn profile – today!

One of the benefits of the LinkedIn job board is that you'll be able to apply for any job you see using your LinkedIn profile. It makes the whole process very easy and enables simple tracking of the positions that you have applied to through the site. Of course, we do recommend maintaining your own separate job application spreadsheet as well so you can see at a glance what companies you have applied to and avoid any unnecessary duplications or confusion.

Indeed

Indeed (www.indeed.com) is another useful resource to help you in your internship search. With Indeed, you have the ability to set it up for daily reminders and daily word searches for particular internships. For example, if you want to work at Facebook, Google, Microsoft, or Amazon, you can set up an alert for each of the different companies and have the list of suitable internships forwarded directly to your email account on a daily basis. That way you are one step ahead of the pack and are notified immediately as soon as the positions are uploaded.

If you make a practice of doing it every day and apply for them as soon as they appear, then you will be better positioned than if you sat down to do it once a week. Applying for suitable jobs needs to be a priority. If you are organized regarding your workload and commitments, then you should be able to fit it into your daily routine.

By diversifying your attention over more than one or two websites at a time, you get to see with clarity which companies are seeking internships regularly and what they are looking for. Note each position down on your spreadsheet as soon as they appear. After you have applied (which ideally should be the same day), then jot down when you sent in your application, resume or cover letter. This will ensure that you don't confuse any job advertisements or forget to apply for them.

Once you have filled in your online profile on the various job boards, make sure to set up email reminders wherever possible to catch all the positions you are interested in. It pays to create a separate spreadsheet where you list the company job application pages, the website name, and the password and username for logging in. It is your well-honed systems that will make the application process run smoothly, and ensure you don't miss out on those first-class opportunities.

Your systems and time management ability will enable you to apply for a large number of positions in a short amount of time. In addition to internships, there are other things such as scholarships, awards, conferences, travel, and fellowships. Skillful organization is the key to balancing it all and coming out on top.

Creating a lifestyle or routine that helps you to apply for internships is just as relevant as getting your name out there. If you can apply for a broad range of internships on a daily basis and streamline that application process, then you will be more effective than 95% of the people that are searching for a job. Your efforts will result in more interviews and an overall higher success rate.

Of course, much of it comes down to being consistent and having competent organization techniques. Being able to take all the application materials and the strategies that we have talked about and put them to the test will ultimately define your success rate. It is imperative that you never give up on the search and keep your eyes on the game. Failing to look or even applying for applications for a week or two could lower your success rate dramatically.

Top Tips to Landing That Kick-Ass Internship

1. Don't sit around waiting for them to fall into your lap

Waiting will not get you anywhere. If you don't apply to online applications or attend every meetup and job fair, then there is very little chance of you finding an internship at all. You have to make an effort and keep an eye out for every opportunity.

2. Be ready

You could stumble upon an opportunity later today, tomorrow or next week. If that does happen, are you ready? Are your resume and cover letter up to date? If you found the ideal position today, do you have everything prepared to send off your application? If not, make it your priority to be ready.

3. Spelling and grammar counts

While you may not pay much attention to your spelling or grammar, note that your prospective employers will. If grammar or spelling is not your forte, then find someone who has strong skills in that area and ask for assistance. A simple spelling or grammar error will reduce your chances of getting an interview; more than one mistake, forget it!

4. Talk to everyone

Chat with everyone you know and everyone you don't. Socialize, mingle and make it your aim to talk to as many people as possible when attending your next event. Consider it your own version of the parlor game, Six Degrees of Kevin Bacon — you just never know who is connected to who unless you talk to them. You just might be pleasantly surprised.

5. Put in the effort

The best results are achieved through hard work and determination. The same applies here. Do your research, look at every avenue possible and keep your mind open to potential companies that might fit the bill. If you put a bit of effort into the task, every day, then it will pay off in dividends.

6. Let your passion show

If you are keen for the position and demonstrate that you want the job, then you are halfway there. Your GPA is not as relevant as people think and your passion will win them over every time, provided you can showcase it in your application as well as the interview. Let them see how you go out of your way to tackle projects and are motivated to see something through to fruition.

7. Start as early as you can

Finding an internship should be on your mind as soon as the first semester begins, even before actually. You can never be too organized when it comes to researching those companies and trying to determine where your future lies. We know it is an exhilarating time as there are so many opportunities ahead. It's all about making the most of them and applying for as many as possible. Larger, more competitive companies will start posting for next summer's internships at the end of the summer, so make sure to enable email notifications to get them sent to your inbox.

When you have carried out all of these actions, you can be confident that you are maximizing your visibility as much as you can.

Your search efforts should, by rights, leave no stone unturned. Scour the websites and be familiar with what is happening in your industry on a daily basis. Talk to everyone and make those conversations count.

At the beginning of your career, it pays to blanket the industry with your applications to get some experience under your belt. Any experience is good experience at the start. Over time, you will start to notice the companies and departments that you have a preference to work in, which will allow you to decide where your interests lie.

Following this chapter, we are going to look at how to use spreadsheets to your advantage as well as how to produce some quality referrals. These techniques will put you ahead of anyone else who is applying through the websites alone.

Chapter FAQs and Action Items

Where can I find more internships to apply to?

Basically wherever you can! To help shortcut the process, look for established and lengthy lists online. Use Google to search for topics such as the top tech internships, greatest places to intern, best places to work, top 100 companies for millennials, etc. Do you get the idea? Look at Vault (www.vault.com) and Wikipedia (www.wikipedia.com); indeed, any website that looks like it could be a valuable starting point, acts as a brilliant source of information and seems relatively up to date.

What is the easiest way to network?

Even if you are a natural introvert, we recommend setting up recurring goals such as reaching out professionally on LinkedIn using a couple of the templates we listed below. Make consistent use of your cold email templates and send them a message to set up a telephone call. Even if it goes against your personality type and speaking to people you don't know causes anxiety, it is still a necessary part of the process.

You must make a personal connection, so you become more than just a name in an email. You just never know where it can lead. It is your contacts that will get you places more than your grades ever will.

Think about this:

Even if you aren't the top student in the class, getting out and being seen will open many doors.

I keep applying to positions but am not seeing any results. What should I do?

The simple answer is to keep at it. If you have applied for 100, then apply for 100 more, and see what the results are! Perhaps you need to rethink your resume or tweak it a little to ensure you are representing yourself in a favorable light.

Go back to the earlier chapters to ensure that you have added in as much as information as possible. If you are confident it reads well, then apply, and keep on applying until you hear back. It can be incredibly disheartening when you don't receive a response. Keep sending them out until you receive a positive reply and secure an interview.

Action Items – 3 Hours

Substantial research and practice will make perfect when it comes to searching for suitable positions.

1. Create a spreadsheet to list all the companies that you want to apply to. We talked about this in an earlier chapter.

2. Set up recurring job notifications that will get sent to your inbox every single day and apply, apply, apply! This is the only way you will succeed! We recommend doing it on a daily basis once you have everything in place.

3. List all companies that you think you might want to work for. Find out if they offer internships and add them to your spreadsheet.

4. Fill out the job application spreadsheet we put together for you so you can stay on top of your systems and processes. Start sending out cold emails as well using our templates.

   Cold Email Template:
   (www.internblueprint.com/resources)

5. Look up any information sessions, career fairs or alumni events happening at your school and make it a priority to go to them.

6. Strip your resume of all your personal information and upload it to popular job boards like Indeed and Monster. You never know what kinds of opportunities are out there! You could just land an internship by being seen in the right place at the right time. Sometimes, it just happens without you having to make much of an effort.

Chapter 5 – Applying to Internships

Now that you have a long list of companies you would like to intern at, it is time to apply. At first, you'll be tempted to take the easy route and submit your resume online to each company. This is a mistake. Online applications are the worst possible way to apply for a job. Like we talked about in Chapter 3, it is not even guaranteed that recruiter will look at your online application. In this chapter, we will explain the methods of applying that can literally double your chances of getting an interview.

These strategies are going to include proven methods such as:

- Referrals
- Cold emailing recruiters
- Informational interviewing/cold referral
- In-person meetups
- Online applications

Referrals

The smartest way to get an internship or land a job is to network. Your friends, colleagues, fellow students – actually any connection you make, no matter how tenuous - should be utilized to your full advantage. Did you know that 85% of jobs are found through networking? That is an incredible number, particularly in light of the fact that the majority of people seeking internships are applying online.

Don't limit your success by focusing all of your efforts on one area. Even if your fellow students spent all their time applying to the online sites we covered earlier, their hit rate is still not going to be as high as yours because they aren't using any of the other methods.

When it comes to referrals, again, don't look to just one source. There are many ways to score a worthy referral. Bearing this fact in mind, let everyone you can possibly think of know that you are seeking a lucrative internship. Get the word out at local organizations such as clubs and activities, and talk to upperclassmen who might be able to refer you. Going through a recruiter and emailing them further down the track may work too.

An employee who subsequently refers you to a company will get a bonus after you have been hired. If you look at it like that, then it's a very highly incentivized way for employees to hand over your resume. They gain nothing by not passing it on and could score a pretty bonus for very little work. So, why wouldn't they? As long as you are professional and polite and will do no harm to their reputation, then you will find that they will be only too pleased to recommend you for an internship position.

Don't discount your friends, family and family friends, too. They may know someone who works at a tech company or another relevant firm that can give you a referral as well.

Ask everyone. Put the word out there – in any and every direction. A lot of people get their initial start through referrals and keeping your job search a secret will not benefit you in the slightest.

Cold-emailing Recruiters

Once you have spoken to all and sundry in your immediate network, then it is time to widen your contact list. When you are considering cold emailing or messaging recruiters on LinkedIn, add them first by sending a personalized message. Look at companies that may be a superior starting point and add them to your list of contacts. This way you can connect with them following a networking event and open up the conversation. Say, for example, you meet a Google recruiter that could be of use to you later on. By adding them to your LinkedIn contacts, you can message them at your convenience when you happen to see a position advertised.

Don't think for a moment that recruiters don't get inundated with messages on LinkedIn. They do, and it is quite a process for them to weed through the vast number of emails that hit their inboxes daily. Therefore, it's essential to keep your messages short and to the point. If you do happen to meet them in person at an event, getting their direct email address will be slightly more efficient because they are more likely to use that a primary source of contact, over and above LinkedIn. Use the cold emailing templates we will provide later on to reach out!

Informational Interview/Cold Referral

You can email individuals such as small random CEOs or companies within your local area that do engineering work or something that is of interest to you. They may skip much of the recruiter process and do some of the hiring internally. Don't be timid about increasing your contacts. Again the worst-case scenario is that they will say no or don't reply at all. Nothing to lose, everything to gain – remember! Use different prospector tools, such as Slik (www.slik.ai) or Email Hunter (www.hunter.io) may be able to turn up a couple of valuable email addresses that you can use to your advantage. We will list a some of the different cold email templates and resources that you can look at below. The main thing is to try and get that personal connection to call in an internship or non-paid internship later on.

Another way to get a personal referral inside of one of your target companies is to go through LinkedIn and filter out people from that company who are similar to you in some way. Similarities could come down to your connections, groups that you're in, or companies that you're following. Maybe you're in the same fraternity as them, or perhaps they are alumni members from your college. Think of yourself as a bit of a detective and see what you can discover. You should be aware that this type of investigative work can be quite time-consuming. Therefore, we only recommend you do it for the companies that are at the very pinnacle of your list.

This is another situation for which it's helpful to have some form of prioritization inside of your spreadsheet. Find a couple of contacts in prime organizations and look for their email address or message them directly through LinkedIn. An email address will be more effective than a LinkedIn message; but if that's all you've got at your disposal, then use it.

From there you message them and say something along these lines:

"Hi, my name is _____ and I was wondering if you were free for a 15-minute phone call to just let me know a little bit more about your company, what you do and how you like your job."

Not everyone will respond, of course, but that's natural. Some people are just too busy to answer, and that's okay. If you can aim for 1 out of 4 to hit an average of 25%, then you are doing pretty well. Even if you only message ten people, hopefully, 2 or 3 will get back to you and want to discuss your situation in more detail.

For ease, we have listed a selection of email scripts below which you can use as a guide. Just copy and paste them into your applications when you need them and amend the company name and other details, so it is specific to your situation. Your confidence will increase with experience.

You need to make sure you follow up with that phone call you mentioned in your initial email or LinkedIn message. 15 minutes is all you need; take a deep breath and dial that number. Ask about the company, what they do there, as well as any other questions that you might have. Let them do the talking. Try not to talk about yourself or distract the conversation away from them. And whatever you do, don't ask for a referral during your first conversation. Keep the focus entirely on them. If they do happen to ask you, you can offer up a little bit about yourself just to be polite, but then try to get the conversation back on to them. Thank them for their time at the end of the discussion and then leave it there.

This is where the importance of your organization skills comes in. You will need to make a note that you called them and then add a date for a follow-up email in a week or so. Once the date arrives, send an email thanking them for their time and letting them know how much you enjoyed the chat. Keep it casual but polite.

Now make a note on your spreadsheet to email them back in about two weeks' time. Let them know that you have been thinking a lot about the conversation and that you have been doing some independent research about the company. Emphasize that you like the sound of what they offer.

Something along the lines of this would work well:

"I enjoyed talking to you, and I think that your company would offer a great working environment for me to gain some experience. I would appreciate it if you would be able to pass on my resume to your HR department. I'm looking for a _____ job, and this would help me in my search immensely".

This is a bold, yet rewarding, way to make connections with companies that you have no previous contact with. You have to be willing to adopt the odd calculated risk or two, to move forward. By making the first move, you have opened a door that was not there before and started to develop a relationship with someone from within.

Another useful option, if you do want to learn more about the company is to search for people who worked there in the past. This is especially helpful as ex-employees will have no hesitation in telling you things that they did not like. You get a more balanced perspective – the good and the bad. An employee currently working at the company may not be so willing to let you know any issues they may be experiencing which prevent you from making a poor choice. Consider this research.

From a referral perspective, however, you want people who are still at the company to pass your resume on to an internal member of staff, particularly in the recruitment or other decision-making arenas.

In-person Meetups

Applying in person at conferences, career fairs, information sessions and hackathons will enable potential employers to put a face to the name on the resume in front of them. It is always worth attending as you never know which companies may be participating. You don't want to miss out on opportunities by skipping a career fair in favor of another event.

When you go to one of these events, aim to get there early - as soon as the event starts, or perhaps right after lunch. This ensures that the recruiters are going to be much friendlier and open to passing on your resume. If you get there just before lunch or just before the end of the event, then they may have had enough at that point and already have their mind on other things.

Bring your well-practiced elevator pitch and work on it some more. If you need practice, use your speech and direct it to companies that are low-priority. Then you can work your way up to the ones you do care about. After two or three goes, you will start getting into the swing of things and develop an easy pattern.

So how should you approach them?

After you have given them your elevator pitch, which should be almost perfect or well on its way to perfection, then hand them your resume. This will ensure that you're going to stand out and be in the top 10% of the people that they meet at the event. Being able to deliver your pitch and back it up with a quality resume will result in a higher chance of them passing on your resume to their HR department.

Although in-person meetups are not necessarily as rewarding as getting an inside referral, it's still a very methodical way to find a job and is certainly on par with cold emailing recruiters.

Online Applications

Sending online applications will undoubtedly increase your success rate, and you will likely score many interviews as a result. When sending in your application material, you need to go through it and individually customize your resume and cover letter to that specific industry.

You must tailor your resume, cover letter or application form to each of the different positions and companies that you're applying to, to make the most of these opportunities. Companies can tell at a glance when your CV is generic – they receive hundreds, if not thousands, of applications for each position and their HR department can spot them a mile away. Find your way to stand out from the others.

Admittedly it can be a time-consuming process, but it is one action that will incur positive results. Show them how well you fit the position and the job description. Leave nothing to their imagination.

Always go through it with a fine-tooth comb after you have edited it to make sure that it is error-free and represents you in a good light. Check each application thoroughly for grammar and spelling and if you have time, have someone look at it for you as well. Often an unbiased person can spot an error you have missed just by giving it a quick glance.

It's often helpful to have a couple of different resume and cover letter options available when applying online. Remember that need to overcome the applicant tracking systems that we covered in an earlier chapter? It will definitely be relevant here. So, make sure that everything is customized for each application and includes all the keywords, software and essential job specific details to get past the computerized system.

Jobscan (www.jobscan.co) can be a very resourceful tool to help you with the process. Basically, it will go through and parse your resume while comparing it to the original job description. It can save you time and help you figure out how to customize your resume. Jobscan can potentially increase your chances of getting a call back; when you look at it like that, it is too beneficial a tool to overlook completely. It can be particularly constructive when you are starting out and force you to look at the job application in more detail.

We recommend that you apply for three different companies and all the various internship positions or full-time positions that pop up in your email feeds every single day. Yes, you heard us right: every single day.

This pattern of agreeable behavior will enable you to get into the habit of applying for jobs and getting your name out there. Remember to add as much information as possible to enhance your resume and character, especially if you're a full-time student or are only a couple of years into your career. You don't have to be even remotely qualified to apply – showing interest is a great first step.

You may as well apply to everything you see that you like the sound of because you never know where it's going to lead, who's going to see it or who they might forward it on to. Just because you are not 100% qualified for the position you are applying for doesn't mean it is a waste of your time. They may have another job in mind which they have yet to advertise, and you might be able to jump the queue by being forthright with your applications.

Experience comes in many different forms. Therefore, mention all of your projects and group experience and make it count. Never misrepresent yourself, however. Always be truthful with your words as your resume will be checked and double checked. You will lose any chance of gaining a position within the company if you are caught out in a lie, no matter how small.

Applying online is something that can be difficult to do if you don't make it a regular habit. You need to muster the motivation and stop making excuses. Try to apply for the maximum number of positions every day and update your spreadsheet as you go so you don't double up through carelessness. Always maintain your focus on success.

If you are going to go this route as your main method, you have to be prepared to send out potentially thousands of applications. Yes, that is not a typo, in the authors' freshman years, they sent out more than three thousand applications combined before securing internships for the summer. If you don't go to a very prestigious school or you don't have prior experience, you should expect the same.

This means that habits and efficiency are going to be incredibly important. If you can get your efficiency to something like ten applications in thirty minutes, and you make a habit of doing this once a day, you will have applied to over a thousand internships in a bit over three months.
Your biggest gains in efficiency are going to come from autofill and batching.

The majority of online applications are going to be of the same few formats. This means that you can use a browser's autofill extensions extremely effectively to save yourself a lot of typing. Download whichever one you like and start applying to places on your spreadsheet. For each new format, it will pull the information entered into its database and make it available the next time you apply to a company using the same format.

Filling in an application on a website is only going to take a couple of minutes at the most if you already have everything copied and pasted into Evernote (www.evernote.com). Don't be in such a hurry, however, that you miss out on following their instructions. They are there for a reason. By failing to follow directions, your resume will end up in the wastepaper bin, regardless of whether you have the necessary qualifications to do the role.

If you think you should have received an answer after sending in 50 applications, then think again. Imagine how much your success rate will improve if you are sending out 50 a day. If you want to increase your success rate, then you MUST find time to do it every day. Spend an hour or two applying to whatever positions and companies come across your desk. This will help you get a feel for what works and what doesn't. From here, you can make adjustments to your resume and cover letter as well as other application materials that you have and parse your way through to success.

The vast majority of your peers will randomly pick 10-20 companies to apply to, send in online applications, and then complain about how tough the job market is when nobody responds. As you can see, there is a much more systematic, intelligent way to go about applying to jobs via referrals, recruiting events, and cold-emailing. And even if you do have to go the online application route, you know how to implement a system that will make applying to over a thousand internships as easy as brushing your teeth every night.

Tips and Tricks

By now your spreadsheet should be starting to fill up and look very extensive, yet organized. It should contain all of the companies you want to apply to, along with the links to application instructions. It's helpful to have another column for referrals and possible connections to the company, as well as how badly you want to work for this company. If you deem it necessary, you can go through the extra hassle of assigning actual numbers on areas such as compensation, location, and the type of work the company is doing. This may help you to analyze how much you want to work at this company. This is a useful way to prioritize which company to apply to first and can assist you with your decision making if you do get multiple offers.

You can also search on Google for topics such as the "list of the 100 top companies to work for" to learn more or go to Wikipedia and search the "list of all consulting companies."

You may have preferences on your favorite method to apply for internships but utilizing ALL of the ways we discussed will help your chances. A personal referral is advantageous, but it can sometimes work out to be the most time-consuming. Skipping one of the methods for another may mean that you miss out on a possible job opportunity. Imagine how bad you will feel if a fellow student landed an internship at the company of your choice; and all because you failed to attend a company information session or email a recruiter! That is not a story you want to tell, so don't make it happen!

Some people struggle to understand that the hit rate for internships is not very high. Even if you happen to be the most ideal candidate, there are going to be many companies that won't get back to you. The position may have already been filled, and if this is the case, then you will hear nothing back. You may not even make it past the ATS which means that your resume will not even get a chance to be seen by human eyes. Other companies may be just so unorganized that you get overlooked immediately. Sometimes, there is no rhyme or reason.

To increase your success rate, don't just apply for ten positions or even 100. This will barely register one or two replies. You need to be applying to multiples of hundreds, especially if you lack experience. You may not get replies for a while, but they will come - especially with continued persistence and a willingness to learn and improve.

Keeping your spreadsheet accurate and updated should be at the top of your priority list. That will help keep you organized and ensure the momentum is there when you are applying for the positions. Don't forget to keep tabs on individuals that you might want to reach out to on LinkedIn as well. Note it in your spreadsheet and calendar when you send them your resume and then make sure you follow up if necessary.

Positions that are offered by recruiters change regularly. If you don't hear anything back after three months, then send in your resume again...and again...and again. Same applies to online applications. You may feel as if your applications are getting lost in the system, and possibly they are. As less than 5% of employers reply to applicants and let them know their applications were unsuccessful, you are left guessing as to a) whether they received it, b) if you made it past the robots or c) were just unsuccessful in your application for whatever reason.

Rather than play the guessing game, give them a call. You may feel hesitant about following up on each application, but even just a short, sharp message will serve its purpose. Just ask them politely whether they have received your application. Nothing to it!

The lesson here is to be organized and stay organized. Don't let your habits lapse out of dismay or due to constant rejection. It is your continuous perseverance that will ensure you get an internship. If you haven't already, then set up the email notifications from Indeed, LinkedIn and other recruitment portals to advise you of all the new jobs as they crop up. Most of them will have the ability to do that, so use it. It will save you from having to go to each site, each day and trawling through the list of jobs.

Once you have had some interest and considered your options carefully, then you don't have to be so aggressive with your applications. If you hear nothing back after a series of interviews, then chalk it up to experience, and start all over again with the process.

Chapter FAQs and Action Items

How many jobs should I apply to every day?

The answer is as many as possible. Literally, as many as you can send out in one sitting over an hour or two every single evening. Do it at the end of the day once all your other work is out of the way and you can apply uninterrupted. Put your favorite music on in the background for motivation and get down to work.

Once you've gone through enough applications, it's just a matter of repurposing what you've already done for each additional application. You can time yourself and stop when your hour or two-hour limit is up and then start again the next night.

How do I motivate myself every single day to apply?

Motivating yourself may take some practice. Some days you may not feel like sending out one application, let alone 20, or even more. But to get anywhere, you must. Just focus on your priorities, and what it is that you want.

Understand your vision as well as your goals, and take the necessary steps to get there. Walk the steps! One foot, after another, after another...one application, after another, after another! Then keep going some more!

If you can manage to send out applications at least four times a week, then you are winning and have more chances than those who only do it once or twice a week. You want to get a head start on the others and land the lucrative spots before they do. Small steps will lead you to your ultimate goal of getting a placement to write home about.

Action Items – 2 Hours

Recall once again that 85% of all jobs are filled by referrals. By now, you see that applying online is a trap. It makes you feel like you have accomplished something, but you most likely have not. There is still no substitute for getting in touch with the right people.

1. Start applying for jobs using the template we provided earlier. Make sure to keep all your resume and cover letters in Evernote, or some similar program, so you have quick access to copy and paste them each time. This will improve your momentum.

   Cold Email Template:
   (www.internblueprint.com/resources)

2. Download your LinkedIn contacts to a CSV and pick out the ones you want to reach out to for informational interviews or a referral. Not all will respond, but keeping your network up to date will definitely have its benefits in the future. You won't regret it.

3. Create a series of standard cover letters and resumes for particular industries. When a possible position comes up, you will be prepared.

Now that things are falling into place, you will be keen to see results. It may not be tomorrow, or next week, but eventually you will get replies which will lead to interviews and internships. As we mentioned at the beginning of the chapter, it is a numbers game, but with some hard work, you can turn it to help you out in the long run.

So keep sending out those applications and keep checking the websites on a daily basis. It pays to remain positive and focused on your efforts. Any lapses due to resentment or frustration can really throw you off your game. The only way to be successful is to be consistent. You've got this!

Chapter 6 – Interviewing

Congratulations! If you have made it to the interview stage, you have been trying hard and doing things the right way. This usually means that you would have by now received an email back from a recruiter saying that they would like to schedule an interview with you. You have every right to feel proud. All of your hard work up to this very point has paid off! Now you have to really execute to get that internship.

Out of all the steps to getting an internship, interviewing is the one least dependent on luck. If you study for interviews, you WILL do better. Technical interviews are very formulaic and thus learnable.

Generally, the process will go something like:
- Coding challenge and/or phone screen
- 1-2 Phone technical interviews
- 2-4 on-site technical interviews (sometimes)

In this section on interviewing, we are going to cover the general process that almost every single company is going to go through before they give you an offer. There will be small differences between each company as they all have their own set of standards to adhere to. But all will expect you to attend at least one interview before they hire you. That much is guaranteed at the least.

Companies such as Uber and Twitter like to send out a coding challenge even before the interview stage. The challenge is designed to filter out those applicants who are not competent in their skills. They do it to everyone regardless of their experience, so try not to take it too personally. Higher-end companies receive a larger number of applicants for each position, so you can imagine that this small test will end up weeding out a lot of people. Similar to coding challenges at career fairs, usually these tests are targeted towards basic technical understandings. By reading *Cracking the Coding Interview*, by Gayle McDowell, you should have a good understanding of what they are looking for and hopefully enough practice to be prepared to succeed.

Once you make it past the initial coding challenge, then you will be asked to do a simple phone screen. This won't be too technical so don't get too worked up about it. You will be asked some pretty standard questions about your skills and experience. The recruiter will just want to run you through your paces and see that you have the knowledge they are seeking.

Again, this is their way of filtering out those who are not qualified. They also want to check that you have sufficient communication skills to get the job done and to see whether you would fit in well with the company. Like the coding challenge, not all organizations will think this step is relevant. They may choose to jump straight into the behavioral interview stage. The first step will be a phone screen. The phone screen is designed to probe a variety of different areas, including interests, what you are looking for, skills you have, general knowledge about the company and position you are applying for.

After your initial telephone screening, you will then be scheduled for a behavioral interview. This will predominantly be conducted over the phone. In some cases, they may request to fly you out for a face to face interview where you will have to sit through a full behavioral and/or technical interview in person. Again, there will be some variation in the way they carry out the steps. Also, not every company will conduct a technical interview; this will be dependent on the internal processes of the particular hiring company.

If you think that there may only be one interview involved before they employ you, then you might be in for a bit of a shock. While it is possible to land a job on the back of one interview, it may also take up to five interviews before you get a final response, either positive or negative. Each call back is another step closer, so you should feel pleased if you have to attend multiple meetings with the one organization. Consider it a small win each time.

To help you feel confident and prepared, we will cover each step of the process in elaborate detail. We are going to focus on pre-interview preparation, coding challenges, phone screenings, behavioral and technical interviews, FAQs and the necessary action steps you need to take to increase your success rate. As with every stage of the internship process, there are always things you can do to better your situation, so be prepared for some homework along the way!

Pre-Interview Steps

There are a couple of different steps you should go through before the interview takes place. Follow these, and you will find that you can minimize much of the stress surrounding the interviews and eventually get those offers.

Much of your anxiety will be due to two factors:

1. Not being organized.

2. Not knowing what to expect.

Lack of preparation is the biggest cause of nerves during an interview. So, relax! You are organized and you know exactly what to expect. Eliminating the unknowns will give you the confidence you need to blow them out of the water and succeed.

80% of the interview happens way before you step into the room for your face to face behavioral interview or get on the phone with your recruiter. It all comes down to your pre-interview strategy, tactics, understanding and other factors. It may involve more than you realize.

Research

Having a good understanding of each prospective employer that wishes to interview you will put you in a strong position. Therefore, your pre-interview strategy should involve creating a document for each company. It is here you will store your research and any relevant information you can find. Consider looking into things such as:

- How long have they been in business?
- What kinds of products or services do they offer?
- Who are their competitors?
- What are their strengths?
- What are their weaknesses?
- How many people do they employ?
- What are the key terms in the job description?

Do a Google search, look at their website and jot down any interesting points that may be pertinent to know in your interview. Look at their latest blog posts if they have one. Read the news section, look at articles on technology websites such as TechCrunch or Forbes, and really familiarize yourself with what they do. Try to fully understand the direction that they are going in the future.

Now consider what will help you get ahead. What may the employer be interested to know about yourself? These questions are a great starting point.

- What are some of the key issues you want to bring up?
- What areas are you particularly skilled in?
- What are your greatest strengths?
- What are your weaknesses?
- How do you think you can add value to the company?

You may wish to jot down parts of your elevator pitch that would be particularly useful. During your phone screening, you can look at this section as a prompt to keep the conversation flowing. Of course, by the time you have a face-to-face interview, you won't be able to take your documentation with you. By then, hopefully, you will have had enough practice and preparation to have your elevator speech memorized by heart.

The expectation during your behavioral interviews is for you to talk about your past experiences, extracurricular activities and projects to show how they could relate to the job you are being interviewed for. Refer back to any industry experience if you have it. If not, you can always discuss topics and experiences that you have had during extracurricular activities, research and personal projects that you have done in the past. Always make sure that you tie it back to the question, make it relevant to your overall character, and as appropriate to the position in question as possible.

On the actual day of the interview, look over your research document. Have it set out with all the research on the company, the different questions that they could potentially ask you, as well as the items that you want to ask them. The information should be noted clearly in one document for ease of access. Look at it the night before the interview, the morning of the interview and during your interview if it is being conducted over the telephone. Reviewing it just before your interview may just enable a crucial fact stick in your mind. This document is vital to your success and preparation.

Draft Suitable Responses

Knowing how to deal with some of the questions that will be asked of you is of tremendous assistance. Let's start with the standard icebreaker, the question we all dread:

"So, tell me a bit about yourself."

Your principal strategy here is to state a few simple facts about yourself. Use your elevator pitch to answer the question but don't be afraid to personalize your response a little. Tell them what you are studying, what projects you are involved in and one or two of your hobbies that will make you sound interesting. You can then delve more into your achievements and experiences that are relevant to the particular job description.

The 'tell me about yourself question' is to ease you into the interview and help you provide quality answers to the questions.

You will also be asked company-specific questions such as *"so why Microsoft?"* or *"what makes you interested in Google products?"* If, for example, you were being interviewed by Microsoft, they may ask you if you can list off all the different Microsoft products that they license out. Random questions such as these are designed to catch you off guard. This is where your corporate research will come in useful. Organizations used to ask more abstract questions to see how you could think through hard problems, such as *"how many golf balls can you fit into a shipping container?"* which nowadays aren't as common as they used to be. Definitely keep your mind sharp for these interviews, as questions like this may pop up. Now, how would you explain the internet to your grandmother?!

You should also expect position specific questions. For instance: if you were being interviewed for a consulting position, then they may ask about your consulting experience or which of your extracurricular activities tie back to this position. It is here you can also talk about any research you have conducted or any past jobs which have some relevance to the interview.

A helpful method which you can use to your advantage is the STAR interview method. This will help you analyze the questions that you may be asked in the behavioral interview to draft a suitable response.

STAR stands for **S**ituation, **T**ask, **A**nalysis, and **R**esults.

Situation

If you were asked this question by an interviewer:

"Name me a time when you had to handle a hard task or a problem within your group. How did you go through and resolve that conflict?"

Your response would first need to specify the situation.

"There was one time when I was working...when this person on my team was not cooperating ..."

Task

Once you have defined the situation and set up the background information, you can then move onto the task and talk a little bit more about what you did. Be specific and discuss various aspects of the job.

"So the task that we were given was to work on a particular database ...it was during this time and we had a little bit of a conflict when doing..."

Analysis

From here, go through and talk a little bit more about how you were able to solve the dilemma or the situation. Describe the skills you used or the particular analysis you found useful.

"Well, I was able to sit down with her and a manager..."

Results

Now sum it all up detailing the final result. How did it end? Were you successful? Was everyone happy? How did you add value to the situation? How will your actions add value to the company you are interviewing for?

"I was able to talk her down and we were able to get on the same page. We were able to work through the issue and eventually were able to complete the project on time."

As you can see you will need quite a bit of practice before you can answer these questions thoroughly. It will be useful to go through all the questions we have listed in the book using the STAR method to draft your response. Then when you have completed those, research some more questions until your answers become second nature. With a bit of study, your answers will flow much easier.

Prepare questions

Feel free to do some extra research to see what other questions may come up, over and above the ones we have listed in this chapter.

Look at Glassdoor (www.glassdoor.com) or Quora (www.quora.com) for potential interview questions. Analyze the questions for relevance. The chances are that you will most likely be asked some of the ones you have covered in your research, or at the very least, something very similar.

It is worthwhile going through each of the questions we have listed and noting several possible answers. Try not to write your answers out in full paragraph style for memorization purposes. Instead, jot down several points, perhaps in a list format, that you might want to touch upon. Your answers will flow more naturally because you have not had to memorize a script.

Making sure that you have your list of questions in front of you is crucial. It may take over 20 interviews before you can adequately articulate what you want to say and how you want to say it. Until then, keep your list of questions with you at all times.

Mock Interview

The last thing to for you to do, is to arrange a series of mock interviews. Use a friend, an acquaintance, or even your career center and go through some of the questions we have listed and those you can source from other websites.

If you have not had any real interviews before, then make sure your list of questions is long. Once you have had quite a large number of practice sessions under your belt, then you will begin to feel more confident about the whole process. At the moment, your aim is a rock solid interview technique, so schedule as many mock interviews as you can before the big day.

Don't forget to practice the technical portion of the interview, particularly when it comes to vocalizing the thought patterns. You have more chances of being called back for a second interview if you come across as composed and confident.

Coding Challenge

Not every company will send you a coding challenge - but don't be surprised if they do. As we mentioned earlier, Uber and Twitter are particularly well-known for it; and there will be others who choose this method to filter out those who are not suitable for the role.

Before the Coding Challenge

Preparation for coding challenges helps in technical interviews and vice-versa. The only real difference is that your code needs to run in a coding challenge but you don't need to explain anything.

The best way to get better at solving coding problems is, unsurprisingly, to solve more coding problems! You can study the theory all you want, but it is much faster to develop an intuition of problem-solving by grinding out as many as possible.

The best resources for coding problems are *Cracking the Coding Interview* by Gayle McDowell and Leetcode (www.leetcode.com). Read through the front matter of CCI first, it contains all sorts of useful problem-solving tips and tricks for these problems. After that, your goal is to solve every single problem in the book. You should write out the full solutions in working code for the first ten or so problems in each section, but after that, it will be enough to write it out broadly in pseudocode.

CCI will give you a good handle on the basics, but to take it to the next level, you should aim to do every Leetcode problem as well. We fully recognize that this is a completely unrealistic goal since you will pass a coding interview and get an offer before getting through every problem. It's a win-win.

We recommend that you dedicate an hour every single day to just solving coding problems. This may seem like overkill, but if you don't do it, you will have wasted all the hours that you spent getting experience, writing your materials and applying to companies. While some people can get by without studying, it is extremely rare and you are probably not one of them.

All the preparation will be worth it when you walk out of a company's office having nailed every single interview and leaving no doubt that you are going to get hired.

During the Coding Challenge

As with any challenge, physical or mental, you will need to warm up. You would be surprised at the number of people who skip this part. Can you imagine running a marathon without doing a warm-up? Or going to the gym and lifting weights without stretching exercises or any physical preparation beforehand? The same applies here! You will need to warm up your brain before even beginning those problematic coding challenges. Coffee may kick-start your brain, but a mental warm-up will give you an edge.

Ease into the exercises gently. Look at the solutions for a couple of the samples. If you think you have time, try to work out one of the solutions from scratch to see if you arrive at the same destination. Consider this your warm up. Now it's time to begin your coding challenge.

You are undoubtedly beginning to feel the pressure right now as there is quite a lot riding on your response. Take your time. Try to stay relaxed. Don't attempt to write out your code solution immediately. Instead, look at the question thoroughly. Write out your general solution. Then go through the problem a second time and optimize it. Don't write the code just yet. You need to have a good idea of the overall solution before you begin writing. Don't rush into an answer that may be incorrect and have you backtracking your thought process.

Write out a simple test case and run your algorithm on it on paper. If it works, you can now start coding it. If it doesn't try a different approach or go back to the brute force solutions.

You may find that this part of the interview has a strict time limit of an hour, or maybe more. The coding challenge can have anywhere between one and four questions that you have to complete in one sitting. Make sure you keep an eye on the clock and finish all the allotted questions in time.

If preferable, you may want to consider looking at all the problems first and begin with the easiest one. This will help you ease into the challenge. Do what you think works best for you, but always keep an eye on the clock as you progress through the questions.

If you don't pass the coding challenge, then you will clearly need to practice your skills in preparation for the next test. Don't be too hard on yourself if you fail. The companies are very experienced when it comes to recruitment, and they do make it quite challenging so that they can hire the best of the best.

Phone Screening

If you managed to pass the coding interview, pat yourself on the back. That is no small feat.

The next stage of the interview is the phone screening interview questions. This will involve a conversation with the recruiter, which can take anywhere from 10 minutes to half an hour. They will ask you a few standard questions about your background and experience and give you more information about the position you are interested in applying for. The recruiter will advise you on the following stages of the interview process and let you know who will be conducting the behavioral interview. A technical interview may also be scheduled, although this does not happen in all cases.

While this part of the interview process is not complicated, you will still need to be prepared. Make sure you have pre-prepared answers ready in anticipation of the questions they will ask you over the telephone. As long as your answers sound professional and coherent, you should not have too many concerns unless there is an unnatural fit.

During the Phone Screen

If you have done your pre-interview preparation, then you should really be ready. Know precisely what the company does, how large they are and how long they have been in operation. The company may even send you a few interview prep questions to help you. If not, then do your research.

Here are some of the questions we have encountered during our interviews. They are very run of the mill and should not pose any issues.

- Tell me about yourself.
- Why do you want this job?
- What is it about this particular job that you like?
- What skills do you have?
- What do you hope to get out of the job?
- How would you describe your work style?
- What is your availability like for interview?
- What are your most significant accomplishments that are relevant to this position?

During the phone screening, you can ask questions. If you wish to clarify anything about the interview process or are unclear about what to expect, then don't be afraid to ask.

Above all; be polite, happy and excited to have been invited to speak to them. After all, not everyone gets to that point. It will help you to stand out, and the interviewer will remember you if you show genuine interest! Always remember that.

Behavioral Interview

Not all companies will hold technical interviews, but a behavioral interview is guaranteed so the hirer can get an idea of how competent you will be in the role. At the beginning of the interview, the manager will run through their agenda and set a time frame so there will no surprises. There may even be a chance to ask questions at the end of the interview so make sure you have them well-prepared.

The purpose of the behavioral interview is to test your knowledge thoroughly. You will also get a chance to discuss your background in more detail as this will be of particular interest to them. Behavioral interviews are based on the idea that your past actions are the most appropriate way to predict how well you are going to handle any role in the future. Therefore, in a behavioral interview, your past actions will come under much scrutiny so the interviewer can establish your skill set.

The first question that anyone will ask you is *"tell me about yourself."* This is a popular choice as a starter question and is just their way of breaking the ice. From there they will ask you company-specific questions and then move on to position-specific questions. Then they will quiz you on your interests and finally will invite you to ask them questions. Interviews can vary in length from anywhere around 15 minutes up to an hour. They can sometimes even be as long as an hour and a half, although it can seem much longer when you are the one being interviewed. If the interview is carried out by telephone, then your research document can become very useful.

You can expect similar questions such as these to gauge your response to specific situations.

- Give me an example of a time where you helped someone without expecting payment.
- Have you ever made a risky decision?

- Have you gone above and beyond the call of duty?
- How do you handle a challenge?
- What would you do if you ever disagreed with a colleague?
- How do you manage tight deadlines?
- Share an example of when you had to motivate someone?
- Have you ever had to prioritize your goals in a work situation?
- How was your transition from high school to university?
- Describe a project that sufficiently displays your analytical skills.
- Have you ever had to make a presentation?
- When was the last time you used your written communication to get your point across?
- What is the most difficult decision you have ever had to make at work?
- Have you ever initiated a project?
- Have you had to solve a difficult problem?
- Has your integrity ever been challenged?
- Describe a situation where you found you had to deal with someone you didn't like.
- Have you ever had a project not go according to plan?
- Tell me about a mistake that you made. How did you correct it?
- Tell me a time when you had to make a split second decision.
- Give me an example of a goal you set and how you set about achieving it.

- What are you most proud of in your career to date?

You should be able to clearly see that these questions differ from the ones you will have been presented with during the telephone screening. And, as you can well imagine, hearing some of these questions for the first time during an interview, can be very stressful. But they are asked with very good reason.

These questions and others like them are used to predict your potential output and how well you're going to complement the team. So, to ready yourself for the behavioral and technical interview, you will need to do your pre-screening techniques we covered earlier. Prepare your stories and adapt them to the relevant competencies that are listed in the job description.

To help you even further, we have included a number of useful resources towards the end of the chapter for you to analyze and familiarize yourself with. The resources will also list 20 questions that you might want to ask your interviewer in case they answer your questions very quickly. Always make sure that you use your allotted time in the best manner possible. Use your interview time to demonstrate that you have a real interest in their company.

Technical Interviews

Before the Technical Interview

Read the section "Before the Coding Challenge" if you have not already. Like we said there, in a technical interview you need to talk through your solution so that the interviewer knows what you are thinking. This is not as easy as it sounds.

Even if you can solve every coding challenge thrown at you, it is not guaranteed that you will succeed once this element is added in. You need to practice specifically for having to explain your thought processes. This means that during at least some of the practice problems you are doing, you should talk through the solutions before and while you are coding them. You might sound like a madman to anyone around you that can hear, but we guarantee that it will pay off later.

For in-person interviews, you will need to be used to writing your solutions on a whiteboard by hand instead of on a computer. This is not as big of an adjustment as going from not talking to talking, but it is certainly something you should incorporate in your practice. Use a spare classroom's whiteboard to write out solutions to your practice problems or just a sheet of paper if that is not an option for you. With these you should also talk out loud and not just in your head when you are coding.

The absolute best way to prepare for technical interviews is to get a group of friends and mock interview each other. Ask each other problems out of CCI or Leetcode and write the solutions out on a whiteboard while talking out loud. The beauty of this is that it nearly simulates the exact scenario of an in-person interview and it gives you the perspective of an interviewer so you know what they are looking for in you.

This is useful for not only in-person interviews, but also for phone interviews. Generally, it is enough to only do the above with friends, but if you want to take it to another level, you can call each other on the phone, open a Coderpad and mock interview that way.

During the Technical Interview

Arrive early, so you have plenty of time to compose yourself before you begin. At the start of the interview, they are going to ask you some very brief standard or behavioral questions. It could be the *"tell me about yourself"* question or one of the other questions we covered earlier. Try to keep your answers brief; you don't need to give your entire elevator pitch here. Save as much time as possible to deal with the technical aspects of the interview.

As we covered earlier in the coding challenge, don't jump straight into the exercise. Hold off on putting pen to paper and writing code. Instead, you need to thoroughly clarify the question before you write down the solution. Draw a picture or go over some test cases, and then start generating an answer.

The first solution you come up with will be a very inefficient brute force solution, possibly without constraints at the end. Once you have analyzed it, you can explain the answer to the interviewer, with the caveat:

"I know that this is not the optimal solution, and it runs in exponential time, which is not going to be the best possible rundown for this. But, the brute force solution is..."

Once you have the brute force solution, then you can begin optimizing. Talk through the process out loud to showcase your problem-solving skills and thought processes. You may want to practice this at home beforehand, so it does not feel strange vocalizing every thought process that is running through your mind. Talking while you're thinking does not come intuitively, so this is where the mock interviews you did before the interview will help you considerably. When you have gone through this process a number of times, it won't feel so alien to you, and it will reduce much of the stress.

The first time is always the hardest. Being relaxed as you are going through the analysis stage will demonstrate to the interviewer that you've practiced these skills and you have no issues solving analytical problems.

After the optimizations are complete and you think you have a well-defined solution, explain it in full to your interviewer. Use the whiteboard if there is one, or, alternatively, the coding platform to simplify it for them. Finally, after you have completed the above steps, you can then begin coding. Once you explain your solution, you should be given a prompt such as *"sounds good, now let's see some code."* This is the magic phrase you have been waiting to hear and you can get down to work.

The coding part of the interview should be pretty straightforward. You should by now have mastered your programming language, and since you know you have a solution they like, it all should go very smoothly.

The coding language you select will come down to two main factors: 1) what you are comfortable in and 2) how widely used it is.

Note the importance of the second point. If you happen to know Haskell exceptionally well, you CANNOT use it if the interviewer isn't familiar with it. It will defeat the purpose entirely. If you are unsure about what programming language to choose, opt for Python since it is the least verbose and most readable. Failing that, use either C++ or Java since they are both widely used in the technology industry.

If a situation arises where you don't find the answer by the time is up, despite your efforts, ask the interviewer for the actual solution. Don't apologize for running out of time; there is no need to verbalize your disappointment. Just move on. Your concern to understand the answer shows them that you don't just care about the solution to get the job. It demonstrates to your interviewer that you care about the answer to further your personal learning, which is a good thing. If you are very close to solving the problem, congratulations; because, that is still a win in their books.

Sometimes these coding challenges have very particular solutions, and they depend on your creativity, experience and knowledge to come up with a specific answer. The interviewers will not nitpick your solution if you didn't get every detail they were seeking. The tests are there to see how much you can work out in the time frame. If you were quite a long way from coming up with the solution by the end of the interview, you could elaborate on why you think you didn't get as far as you had hoped. However, it's not going to matter too much at this point.

Just shake their hand, tell them that it was nice to meet them and head back to the lobby (if it was a face-to-face interview). You may also have a chance to ask them some questions, such as how they like their position or what the next step in the interview process will be. Show them you are still keen to persevere with the job regardless of the results of the technical interview.

Interviewing, whether it's in person, on the phone, technical or behavioral, takes a lot of time and effort to get right. Practicing is the only way to improve. There is no shortcut to being able to interview well. Do round up your friends or ask your career center to help you get familiar to answering unexpected questions through the mock interviews. It doesn't matter what others think about your process, as long as you appear confident and comfortable in an interview setting. Try to mirror an actual interview setting in the mock interviews where possible. You need to practice every single day; this is not something that will come to you naturally or right away.

We have included a template for you to practice your interviewing skills and some questions you should ask the recruiter and hiring managers at the end of your interview. The Interview Prep Template will list additional interview questions to formulate your responses.

Interview Preparation Template & Questions to Ask:
(www.internblueprint.com/resources)

Chapter FAQs and Action Items

Are short interviews a negative sign?

No - they aren't! Depending on which stage of the interview process you are at, the lengths and times are going to vary enormously. Maybe you did terribly. Maybe you did really well. Maybe the interviewer just needed to screen more candidates. Whatever the case, try not to worry about how long the interview ran for! Just try as hard as you can and follow those templates and the advice we gave you!

When should I reach out after interviewing?

Reach out as soon as the interview is over. Send a follow-up note to HR, the recruiter or the manager – whoever it was that interviewed you. If you don't have the person's email, send it to your HR contact and ask them to pass your note on to them. Just a quick and simple message such as, "thank you for your time today, I am excited to hear back from you!" will be suffice.

Action Items – 2 Hours

We can guarantee that if you don't prepare, you WILL do poorly in your interviews. We don't mean to scare you, but just make you realize that all of your previous work is for naught if you don't take the time to study.

Pull up your calendar and schedule one hour early in every single day where you will focus only on technical interview preparation. This may seem like a lot of time, but it will ensure that you are 100% ready for any interviews that fall into your lap.

Interviewing is one of those things that takes a lot of time to get right, so don't be discouraged if you can't get an internship on your first interview. Our methods are backed by real results. Prepare for those questions, speak in front of the mirror, record the mock interviews – do whatever it takes to ease those nerves and appear professional during your interview. If you make a mistake or feel you have put your foot in your mouth when it comes to a particular response, don't dwell on it. Hindsight is a great thing, and you can always use it as a great learning tool for what NOT to do again.

1.   Set up at least two mock interviews. If you have had no experience to date with interviews at all, then more may be necessary. Record it to check your responses and gauge how well you did.

2.   Create your interview template to look over during your phone interviews. To be prepared, you must not skip any of the interview preparation processes as it can mean the difference between success and failure.

Interview Preparation Template & Questions to Ask:
(www.internblueprint.com/resources)

3.   Keep practicing those technical interview questions as well. Try to solve one problem every day to keep you on your toes. Obtain a copy of Cracking the Coding Interview by Gayle McDowell and sign up for a Leetcode account (www.leetcode.com).

Chapter 7 – The Offer

Depending on the company, you may not hear back for quite a long period of time. Unless you heard differently from them during the interview process or via email, wait at least one week before contacting the company regarding their decision. Contact them and ask what the next steps are in the process and if they have any more information to offer.

If they do not get back to you, contact them every week after that, unless they specify otherwise. Some companies take eons to get back to you, so make sure to set up calendar reminders to follow up. Not hearing back can be extremely frustrating. There will be interviews where you don't even hear back regarding the company's decision, which is very unprofessional. Just keep in mind that it happens and keep persevering until you hear back.

When you get your initial job offer, you will be over the moon with joy. Undoubtedly, you will be very keen to accept the first job offer which comes your way. Try to hold off for a moment.

Before you sign on the dotted line, we are going to take you through what you can expect from an offer, the scary negotiation process and how to determine the most ideal internship position for you. The good news is that you don't have to make your decision immediately. The organization will give you plenty of time to make a decision, and you can always ask for an extension if it is required.

What to Expect

The period between your interview and the offer letter can feel excruciatingly long. You will probably find yourself checking your missed messages and emails more regularly than usual. We can totally imagine your excitement when the recruiter or hiring manager telephones you to give you the amazing news – we have both been there! If you received the news by telephone, then they may send a formal letter after the fact to advise you that you were successful in your application and interview. The manager or recruiter may also choose to email you to let you know you have been successful.

The first communication you receive will confirm your success and provide more details on the offer. It will mention relevant facts such as your intended position, hourly rate or salary, the address where you will be working, and the date you will be expected to start. They may advise you of which team you will be working with, recommended office hours, and any expected overtime, although any of these facts could be presented at a later date. They will also mention benefits and perks relevant to the role.

The facts provided in the initial email or telephone call should hopefully be enough for you to base your decision on. If you have any further questions at this stage, don't hesitate to reach out to them. Let any other companies that you have been interviewing with or contacting know that you have another offer as soon as possible. This will allow you to be expedited in the hiring process which can make negotiations much easier later on.

Are you going to accept the job? Maybe! Maybe not! Your decision should not be made lightly, and you will need to take a number of factors into account. If there are some things that you need to negotiate, then now would be the time.

Negotiation

Not every company will let you negotiate, particularly if it is your first internship. But if there is something that is a little concerning about the offer or that you may wish to change, then there is nothing wrong with trying. You can always accept the original offer if they won't budge, provided you haven't been rude or asked for the downright ridiculous. A simple negotiation request will not harm their first offer in any way, and the worst-case scenario is they will say no. At that point, you can decide whether you will take their offer or turn it down in its entirety.

If you get an offer from a top-tier company and have no others on standby, then it may be prudent to accept what is on the table. You have absolutely no leverage for negotiation and the position, as you know, will be in high demand. Just think how much work you had to do to land it in the first place. Throwing that all away on a whim might not be the smartest thing to do. However, if you have two offers and there is something you particularly don't like about one of them, then it would be in your greatest interests to negotiate to see if you can get a better deal.

The most common aspects of the job which tend to be up for negotiation relate to pay, the team, and location. When it comes to the salary, you need to calculate how much you expect it will cost you to live where you will be working. If your expenses exceed your salary or will barely cover your living costs, then present this issue to your recruiter and request more money. If the wage is sufficient, and you don't have another position to consider, it is not worth bothering with a negotiation since you have no leverage.

If you would prefer a different team or even location (if possible), then there may be some flexibility here. Just explain to your recruiter that you would prefer something else. It doesn't hurt to ask, and most of the time they can do something about at least one of the issues. They want you to be happy, after all!

In the case where you do have a secondary offer, you will most likely get some things to tilt in your direction. First, compare the jobs themselves. Which one is at the top of the list? Not having a preference simplifies things somewhat, although, you will most likely have a preference for one company over another for any number of possible reasons. Go back to your initial research if you need to refresh yourself on the particular details of the company.

Now put together a list of all the differences between the two offers. Include everything from the obvious such as salary, team, and location down to the smallest points such as hourly vs. monthly pay and the nuances of a company's reputation.

When it comes to the actual negotiation stage, always do it over the phone. Just explain to your recruiter that you have additional questions you'd like answered and then broach the subject during the conversation. Communicate your specific contract concerns and detail the changes you would like to see happen. Don't be afraid to put in a counter offer to increase the salary by between 5-15% higher than their original proposal depending on how good your other offer is. Some companies can be very inflexible on the salary although perks such as flights, starting bonuses, or a housing stipend can be added to the table for discussion.

For more resources on negotiation, we have put together a list of the best tactics that we've found for you to be successful. Visit the link below and click through to the negotiation section.

Make sure you read them thoroughly! Also, keep in mind that negotiating takes a lot of time and effort. Ask them for an extension on your due date if you think it is necessary to give you extra time to make your decision.

It will also increase your chances of receiving another offer before your time is up. It will be easier to win the negotiation battles if you have more positions to choose from.

Your goal is to choose that kick-ass internship and ideally come out on top. Rushing to accept the first offer could have you regretting your decision in the very near future.

Negotiation Articles:
(www.internblueprint.com/resources)

Choosing an Internship

Being in a position where you can choose between two or more internships is optimal. However, there are a few things that you need to be on the lookout for when you are going through and making the comparisons.

Reputation

The number one thing to look at is the reputation of the company, particularly when it comes to their computer science talent. Consider hedge funds, for a moment. If you get an internship at a hedge fund, then everybody can instantly see that you are talented and ultra-competent – otherwise, you wouldn't have landed the role. Hedge funds only hire the top candidates.

If you're a computer science major, then you also naturally understand quite a bit of math and finance despite your computer major. So, if you can get a placement at a hedge fund – well done – that is on the top tier in terms of reputation, and you should be very pleased.

Companies such as Palantir and Google are a close second when it comes to reputation, followed by Microsoft, Apple, Facebook, Amazon and also top startups like Airbnb and Uber. You will need to determine the reputation of companies outside of this list through your research. Bear in mind that the reputation of these companies, and many others, from a technical perspective, will differ from the opinion of the general public or even your family members. A company may be extremely favorable in the public eye but have a terrible reputation on the technical side, and vice-versa. Speak to your contacts in the field to see what you can learn about any company making an offer before you commit.

Working Environment

The second thing to consider is the working environment. If we use the example of hedge funds again, then it is worth noting they don't exactly compare well to other working environments. While they are good from a reputation perspective, they are often known for overworking their interns.

They also don't have as many perks as other companies such as Palantir or Google. Depending on what your goals are, if you really want to break into quantitative finance, then your priority may be to go with the hedge fund internship. If you are more interested in the working environment and the perks and benefits you receive, then accepting a position with Microsoft or Facebook may be more lucrative for you. Choosing another company over a well-respected hedge fund will not necessarily affect your resume negatively if they still rate quite high on the reputation list.

Learning Potential

While you are working at the company, you should always make continuous learning a priority. 'Continuous learning' may sound a bit vague at the moment, but it is worth asking each organization how they will support your continuing education while you are employed with them. What can they offer you along the lines of study opportunities? It may be that they can provide some sort of mentorship or dual mentorship program. Occasionally you will buddy up with another intern. If you want to make the internship count, then you have to ensure you are going to get the most out of the experience as possible.

If you are 100% sure that a company with a very high reputation is not going to offer much in terms of their working environment or learning potential, you are free to choose an alternative organization. We do recommend you weigh up your decision very carefully, however, as turning down a company with a stellar reputation may not be the most approved course of action.

There are secondary aspects which you will need to take into account such as location and salary. Obviously, all else being equal, you can decide which internship you will select based purely on salary and location. But generally the facts will be pretty clear-cut once you have analyzed their reputation, working environment and learning potential.

You will also need to consider how your internship will ultimately help your career. Just because you are starting on the bottom rung of a ladder, doesn't mean that you can't climb up to the next level to get to where you want to be. If you wanted to work at Google as a developer and couldn't get in as a freshman, then attempt to find something else in the interim. Don't lose hope!

Once you have some real experience, you can slowly work your way up and reapply once your prospects have improved. It all comes down to knowing where you want to work, what sort of companies you are looking for and then making a plan to get there. Don't let your current lack of opportunity stop you from having a goal.

We are confident you will make the best decision. Just look before you leap. Weigh up the pros and cons, the salary, their reputation, the benefits, the company location, the team, the learning opportunities and then choose.

Chapter FAQs and Action Items

How do I know if the pay rate on offer is good?

The answer depends on where you are in your academic field and which field the company is based. Since we're mainly focused on technology internships, for a first-year student, $15 to $25 is a great start. Once you are a sophomore, that number will increase from $20 to $35, or even more. After that, it may rise to $40+ an hour. It will depend on the location of the internship, the industry and a whole host of other factors.

Glassdoor has a wonderful tool, aptly called the Know Your Worth Tool that can give you an idea of your salary: (www.glassdoor.com/salaries/know-your-worth). LinkedIn also has one called the Salary Tool (www.linkedin.com/salary). Visit both links online to see what they put your profession or chosen area of study to be.

What do I do if they say no to my negotiations?

If they say no to a salary increase, it is not the end of the world. You can still negotiate on other factors including your starting bonus, overtime pay, relocation reimbursement, housing and start date. They clearly spent a lot of time, effort and money in recruiting you.

If you turn it down now, they will have lost their entire investment.

Try to remain from being brash or confrontational throughout your negotiation discussions. Remain sincere and friendly, and things will work out. Like we mentioned earlier, there is never a downside to negotiating if you do it right.

When you have made up your mind, it is merely a case of letting the recruiter or manager know over the telephone, followed up with a letter sent by email for clarification. Confirm and acknowledge the terms of the agreement, so there is no room for error and to ascertain whether you are both on the same page. That way if there are any problems or there does happen to be a change in the situation, they will come back to you and advise you of the fact immediately.

If you wish to decline the position, then it is always nice to let them know via a letter or email as well. Thank them for the opportunity and keep all communication between you and the company professional and polite.

Action Items – 3 Hours

1. Spend a few moments reading all the articles that we have provided for you on salary negotiation. These will give you a fantastic baseline to negotiate your salary and other benefits you are looking to receive. Remember, it never hurts to negotiate if you are coming at it from the right angle.

Negotiation Articles:
(www.internblueprint.com/resources)

2. If you have one offer on the table, then email all the companies you have recently had an interview with and let them know. Advise them that you need to make a decision by the said date and ask whether there may be an offer from them shortly. This may prompt them to give you an offer sooner rather than later, and it will give you more leverage in your negotiations.

3. Make a list of the pros and cons for each position. Rank all your offers under the following categories: reputation, work environment, and learning potential. Most likely, your best option is going to be the one that is the best at all of these.

Chapter 8 – The Internship

Once you have accepted the position and secured your internship, then you must get organized to set yourself up for success. You will have a lot to do regarding the arrangement of housing, transport, and everything else that comes with such a move.

Generally speaking, your number one goal in your internship is to get a return offer. The best way to achieve this is to do your job to the best of your ability, seek feedback, and use it to course correct.

Of course, a return offer is certainly not the only thing you can get out of an internship. You can learn both technical and soft skills, meet interesting people that can help you in both your personal and professional lives, and have a ton of fun.

In this chapter, we will present our best tips and tricks for making the most of your internships.

Onboarding

Each company will have their individual onboarding process and will go out of their way to make you feel welcomed as one of the team members. Their early introduction to the company should set you up for future success and give you very apparent expectations and goals to work towards. Their onboarding process should also ease some of the nerves you will be feeling on your first few days. Seek out other interns to befriend if necessary, so you don't feel as alone as you might feel, particularly at the beginning when everything seems daunting and unfamiliar.

Aim for Success

It should really go without saying, but we feel that this book would not be complete without mentioning that the number one most important thing you should do in your internship is a good job. If you have to work extra to get everything done, do it. You should have the mindset that you will get your tasks done, on time, with quality, no matter what.

From the start of your job search to the first day of the job and beyond, success has always been your primary goal. As we have shown you, the steps to success are to break down goals into small, actionable bits that will over time lead to success. The following tips will ensure that you well and truly achieve it, while at the same time demonstrating your worth to your employee.

Be Proactive

The majority of intern projects are going to be under-scoped. If you are able to be efficient with your work, it is highly likely that you will finish your project well before the deadline. Knowing this, at the beginning of your internship, you should work with your manager or mentor to define a stretch goal or two in case. Though sometime you will even finish these before the end of your time at the company!

In cases like these, the majority will just sit around and basically do nothing. You, of course, should do the opposite: take the initiative and ask anyone you can if they could use your help. This will give you an incredibly good reputation, which will be invaluable when it comes time for your manager to make hiring decisions.

Communicate with your manager

A helpful strategy to guarantee success is to document all the things that you do each day. Take a moment at the end of each day and write your list of things you have accomplished, what you spent your time doing, and what you want to get done later on. Doing it on a daily basis, instead of each week, is beneficial, so you don't forget any of the information and makes your list more robust. Make this a part of your daily routine for consistency.

When Friday rolls around, email the document to your manager, your manager's manager, sometimes your manager's manager and update them on how your week has gone. Carbon-copy them all on the same email. Ask them what they think you should focus your efforts on in the upcoming week and if they can offer any advice. This is absolutely crucial in getting visibility from managers and higher-ups.

This strategy will help you on a number of different fronts.

1. It will make sure that you are focused on your work and adding value every single day.

2. It will show your manager that you are capable of working hard and managing your time adequately.

3. It will allow you to keep an itemized list of all the different things you've done during your work experience and demonstrate your value without question.

4. It will provide an opportunity for some useful feedback from your manager as you progress through your internship.

5. It will demonstrate your ability to communicate comprehensibly and most importantly, gain visibility.

This document will come in handy during and at the end of your internship. When you go back and edit your resume, you will have a full list of tasks to go through. Identify and add the information that will stand out particularly well on your resume. How were you able to provide value to the company? Did you work on any particular projects? What did you achieve? It will also give you further topics to discuss in your next interview. Just make sure to communicate with your manager at the end of the internship to check what you can or cannot share with other companies.

It is always helpful to clarify the organization's expectations of you early on in the process. Communicate with your manager regularly and try to keep the communication channels open, regardless of how informal the structure of the company may seem. Your weekly email that you send to management will ensure that you tick all of your boxes. Note that your manager or supervisor may also request weekly and monthly face-to-face meetings for performance checks and feedback. Make sure to have a one-on-one meeting with your manager at least once every two weeks.

Network

Once you finish the internship, you must make sure that you are remembered by your managers and colleagues. This is particularly beneficial when you complete your studies and are seeking a full-time job. To manage this, you need to find a positive way to stand out in their mind and show them just how much of an asset you were during your time with them.

Try to develop a professional, yet personal, relationship with the individuals you work with. Reach out to your boss, their boss, your team members, your colleagues – anyone who you may come across on a daily basis. Get lunch with them, ask them questions about how they got to where they are today. Use your time to network and develop those contacts to help you with your future job search. Having those personal relationships is the key to your success and the expansion of your network.

As well as forming personal relationships with managers and co-workers, you also need to develop your relationships with your fellow interns. This is an area that is very often neglected by interns. They are your peers, and your relationship with them may just lead to a position in the future. Don't ignore anyone, regardless of how unimportant they may seem to you at the time. Treat everyone as an equal and view them all as a potentially valuable asset.

Even after you leave the company, make it a priority to maintain your relationships and keep in touch with your coworkers. A quick email every now and again will ensure you are in their thoughts. Regardless of how much time has passed since you were working in the position, maintaining contact, especially when you are more experienced, is a great way to seek out enriching positions and fantastic opportunities. Having a strong personal professional relationship with colleagues, managers and peers will open doors for you in the future.

Keep busy

When you begin your internship or full-time job, keep yourself as busy as possible. If things are quiet on the work front, then use your initiative and seek out any extra tasks you could do. Your managers and colleagues will be only too happy to give you additional work if it is available. If there is nothing to do, then examine your situation carefully and see where you can add further value to the company.

Ask around if necessary. If, as an example, you're working on a project and you notice it could be improved in some way, then come up with a plan. Talk to your colleagues about their problems and if you can assist them. Always show initiative no matter what happens. Run it by your supervisor before you go ahead and just explain that you have the time to carry out the extra work without it interrupting your regular duties. Side projects and working with other people will help you add value, build those relationships and make you so much more valuable. Don't forget to note your efforts in your weekly documentation to keep yourself accountable.

Showcase tangible results

You want to be able to demonstrate to future employers just how much you achieved during your time with the company. Communicate with your manager at the end of the internship to check what you can or cannot share with other companies. You want to be able to share as much information as possible to showcase your efforts. If some of the information is confidential, then you may need to have two presentations: one you share internally if you are seeking an alternative position within the company and one that you share externally with other unrelated organizations. Work with what you have and make sure you always act in accordance with the corporate guidelines. You can then share your external presentation on your personal website and LinkedIn in the hope that a keen recruiter may stumble upon it.

If you can get your name on a white paper or a research paper while you are carrying out your internship, then it is something you should aim for. Ask around and see what opportunities are available. Are there any extra research projects that would provide a welcome boost to your career? Failing that, try to get a blog post published on their corporate website. This will benefit both the company as well as yourself.

The organization will get to show off their internship program and the young talent they are nurturing; and, it is an impressive way to build up your reputation. Any experience or marketing opportunities are welcome, and again, you can link it back to your website and LinkedIn profile. It is also another tool that a recruiter can use to learn more about you and your experience.

Ask questions

Always ask questions. As an intern, you are expected to get things wrong. But asking questions ahead of time will make the process a lot easier for you and will demonstrate your initiative. Try to learn as much as you can and be as useful as possible. If you want to get ahead, be the intern that proposes solutions rather than the one who reports a problem. See the difference?

As an intern, you are certainly not expected to know everything. You most likely have an assigned mentor on your team that you can go to ask any questions you have. Be sure to take advantage of this, especially when you have company-specific questions.

Keep your eyes open

How can you tell if your internship has a chance of becoming permanent? Our best advice is to keep a close ear to the ground and talk to everyone about your plans. Is the company or department expanding? If they are, there could be a possibility of employment in the future. If your managers and colleagues are aware that you will be looking for a full-time permanent position in the future, then they will call on you if you have proved yourself.

Make the most of your experience

Your internship position will not last forever, so try to make the most of your perks and learning opportunities. Keep your eyes peeled to see what is around and available.

Take advantage of perks

Take advantage of every perk that you can find at your internship. There are a lot of companies that will offer up things like free coffee or food. If they have a fancy espresso machine at your workplace, then learn to enjoy coffee. Happy hours are another bonus. You may also get free bus passes or museum passes. They may even give you funds to cover your travel expenses and safety gear.

Focus on learning

Don't forget to concentrate on furthering your personal learning while you are doing your internship. You may find that your manager is happy to cover the expenses of an online course or individual research in the way of book purchases or other material, provided that it is relevant to your current role. It doesn't hurt to ask your manager directly as this may not have been specified during the interview or hiring stage.

Have fun!

Lastly, don't forget to have fun! You are most likely in a city you haven't been before, surrounded by people you've never met before. Throw a party or barbeque at your apartment, invite all your fellow interns, and tell them to invite anyone they know as well. This is the best way we know of to bootstrap your personal network in a new city.

Make it a point to do something interesting every weekend. Explore the city with your new friends, go hiking on a nearby mountain, eat at cool new restaurants. Your internship is not very long, so you need to make sure you make the most of it.

Chapter FAQs and Action Items

How can I set myself up for a full-time offer?

Positioning yourself for a full-time offer should be one of your goals at the start of an internship, especially if you are entering your senior year of school. During your manager one-on-ones, make sure you keep inquiring about full-time positions. Understand what they are looking for and whether they may be hiring in the next 12-month period. Keep working as hard as you can and demonstrate your excellence and competence to create a good impression. Remember, personal professional relationships are key here.

What should you do when you finish your internship?

There are quite a few things you should do once you have completed your internship. Always thank your manager by email, personal note or even by sending a little gift. This is applicable no matter how long you were at the company in question. There is no need to go overboard. It is just a token of appreciation more than anything. Next, update your resume, LinkedIn profile and personal website by referring back to your weekly updates and progress reports. Ready yourself for the next round of applications and interviews and put yourself in a well-placed position to land another. Even if a lot of what you learnt was not relevant to your future career, the experience is still beneficial. Now, continue to build on your skills while keeping an eye out for projects, research papers and anything you can get involved with. Keep learning, keep applying and keep having fun!

How can I tell if I am doing a good job?

You will know that they are taking you seriously if they ask you for advice or are happy to endorse your work on LinkedIn. Even if they don't come right out and say it, if you get invited to social events such as happy hour, then it's usually a good sign that they are impressed with your work. If you have a professional attitude, are pleased to take on tasks over and above your standard workload, show up on time, dress well, are polite and friendly, then there should be no major concern on this front.

Any final word on internships?

Be yourself, learn as much as you can, act professional and enjoy the moment. Take advantage of the fact that you are in a new geographic area for a limited period with unfamiliar faces. Get to know as many people during your time with the organization and explore your surroundings. You are in a unique position where you can improve your skills, learn new things and get paid without any significant commitment. It is perfect to test out what you like and enables you to define with clarity what you dislike.

Action Items – 1 Hour

This is our last set of action items for the book. We hope you take advantage of them and put them to good use. With all of these steps from Chapter 1 to Chapter 8, you have now set yourself up for the best possible path to success. From a caterpillar to a butterfly, you have emerged from barely being employable to becoming the most employable individual within your class! Remember that everything in this entire book is a process, and processes take time to master, develop and succeed. Take this framework that we have given you and implement it. You will be thankful you did.

1. The first step is to set up a game plan for the internship as well as your list of goals. Beyond

getting a return offer, your list could incorporate such things as learning a new programming language or getting to know a bunch of people.

2. As we talked about earlier, networking is crucial while you are at your internship. Make a plan to get to know x amount of people by the time you are done with your placement and set out to achieve it. If you manage to get to know more than your goal, wonderful!

3. Set up routine 1-1s with your manager and send that summary and accomplishment document every week. The document will be vital in ensuring you remember what you have accomplished, as well as helping you increase your visibility in the organization.

Conclusion

It's been quite a journey, hasn't it? And some days, we are certain, were more difficult than others. We hope you have learned a lot along the way and were rewarded for your all your hard work and determination with a great internship. If you have not been successful yet, then we hope that your offer is just around the corner.

Let's recap on what we discussed throughout the book.

We took you through the specifics of what internships are and the different types of opportunities out there. Then we focused on laying the foundation that would allow you to get to the first stage and stand more than a fighting chance of getting an internship. With these experiences under your belt, you could put together the resume, cover letter and elevator pitch that would get you to the next step; finding and applying for internships.

Through your actions and by adhering to the best practices, you are guaranteed to land yourself an interview, or two (or even more). From here, we moved on to the interviewing section. We walked you through the best strategies for interviewing and outlined some of the more important things you need to keep in mind before you receive your offer. Next, we covered what to expect from your offer, how to choose the best offer and how to negotiate the best deal. Then in the final chapter, The Internship, we touched on how to succeed during your tech internship and how you can use what you learned to propel your career forward.

We hope you have found all these strategies, templates and resources extremely helpful and we wish you the best in your search for the most exciting and rewarding internship you can get! There is no denying that we made plenty of mistakes during our internship process and we just wish that this information was available when we were looking to land our first internship.

But, needless to say, it wasn't — so we took it upon ourselves to fill that knowledge gap and share what we learned with others. It is in this book, Tech Intern Blueprint, and our supporting information that you can learn directly from our mistakes, save time and reduce stress when it comes to the tech intern search.

What many don't realize until far too late is that what you do during college sets up the rest of your life and by now you know that internships are among the most important things that you can do during these years. The strategies that we have covered are your path to an extraordinary internship, which will serve as the first step on your journey to an extraordinary life.

If you want to learn more, then make sure you visit our website at College Hustlers for up to date blog posts and relevant information (www.collegehustlers.com). We have also created a Facebook page called Tech Intern Blueprint which will provide continuous updates, more advice, and even a few success stories (www.facebook.com/techinternblueprint).

Best of luck for today, tomorrow and the future!

Cheers,

Ray Parker
Charlie You

P.S. For even more resources, including checklists, templates and examples, worksheets, and one-pagers, visit: (www.internblueprint.com/resources)

Chapter Summaries

The Tech Internship Blueprint Core Principles

1. Getting job offers is a learnable skill.
2. Never give up. It is NEVER too late.
3. Consider the company's point of view.

Chapter 1 - Internship Overview

- An internship is a job that is relevant to your field of study typically done during the summer break.
- There are different types of internships depending on when you do it, how long it is, whether it's research or in the industry, what your role is, etc.
- Benefits of internships include being able to try out different roles, companies, technologies, etc., gaining experience and skills, getting paid, and meeting people.

- Think of an internship as the first stepping stones in your career: the better internships you have, the better full-time job you will get.

Chapter 2 - Getting Experience

- The best experience is past internships, but assuming you don't yet have any, you should get as much experience as you can from classes and independent studies, research, and personal projects.
- Choose classes that are relevant to your field in terms of both subject matter and material type (theory vs practice).
- Research is recommended for everyone, but essential if you want to go to grad school. Find out which professors are doing cool research and go talk to them.
- Independent studies are a great way to earn credit by doing a cool project with a good professor. Bonus: not many people do them, and it shows initiative.
- If you can't get anyone to give you credit for a project, do it anyway! Make it open source and blog about it. Treat it as important as your classes and research.
- Seek out extracurricular activities and clubs to have fun and potentially gain leadership experience.

Chapter 3 - Marketing Materials

- You need to put together a resume, a set of cover letters, a LinkedIn profile, a website, and an elevator pitch.
- If your marketing materials are not good, you WILL NOT get interviews. Almost no one spends enough time getting these right.
- Resume: keep it to one page, use a simple and consistent format, include quantitative results, get it reviewed by someone who knows what they're doing
- Resume says what you've done, cover letter says why what you've done is relevant to the company. Be enthusiastic and confident. Write one cover letter for each type of company you are applying to (finance, social media, etc.)
- Elevator pitch will be used at career fairs, info sessions, and networking events. Base it off of your resume and cover letter and practice it until you can do it under stress.
- LinkedIn is your extended resume online.
- Setting up a simple website is easy and has enormous benefits. Use it to show off your design and coding skills as well as blog about personal projects.

Chapter 4 - Finding Internships

- List every company that you've ever heard of that you might want to work for. Go online to see if they offer internships.

- Find additional companies to apply to on your school and public job boards and through networking at info sessions, events, career fairs.

Chapter 5 - Applying to Internships

- By far the best way to apply to a job is through an employee referral. Use LinkedIn to see if you know anyone or can get an introduction. Ask friends and family. Seek out school alumni. Do anything and everything. 85% of jobs are obtained via a referral. We cannot emphasize the superiority of referrals enough.
- If you cannot get a personal referral, you can cold email employees and try to get a referral that way. Often companies will incentivize them. This does, however, take more work than knowing someone.
- The second best way to get a job is by cold emailing recruiters or going to a career fair. The end result is the same: a recruiter is guaranteed to look at your resume, but you don't have the endorsement of an employee referral.
- Applying online is an order of magnitude worse than the above two methods. The only upside is that it is easy to spam applications, which might be necessary your first year.

Chapter 6 - Interviewing

- If you do not prepare, you WILL fail. All the work you've done to get the experience and present it well is wasted if you do not adequately prepare for your interviews.

- Possible steps in the interview process: coding challenge, phone screen, phone technical, on-site technical. Companies will combine these steps in different ways.

- To prepare for behavioral questions, outline responses to the most common ones and practice saying them out loud.

- To prepare for technical questions, do a lot of them. Buy Cracking the Coding Interview and do all of the problems. After that, do every problem on Leetcode. Easier said than done. Get into the habit of spending time each day on it.

- Always prepare questions to ask your interviewer as well.

- Get a friend and mock interview each other. These are more helpful than you might think.

- Get enough sleep the night before your interview.

Chapter 7 - Internship Offers

- Information that you will need to make a decision: what team you will be on or the team selection process if it is not decided yet, where you will be, how much you are paid, if you need to pay for housing

- Prioritize learning over money over the location. Reputation vs learning is more nuanced.
- If you want something changed, negotiate for it. Most likely you won't get it, but it is good practice and there is no downside for trying.

Chapter 8 - The Internship

- Your goal during the internship is to learn as much as possible and get a return offer (assuming you want one).
- Mature intern programs will contain lots of structure. If yours does not, work with your manager to create some.
- Do not be afraid to ask questions. Be proactive and seek out the opportunities that you want. Network. Constantly seek out feedback and adjust as needed. Be professional and get your work done.
- If you get your day-to-day right, the return offer will take care of itself.

Appendix

Our bonus section, provides additional information that we believe you will find extremely helpful. Everyone's background may be different, but it is up to you to position yourself well using your unique talents and skills. Don't let anything impede your search or stand in your way.

At the beginning of the internship process, you will feel that there are many hurdles ahead. Take each hurdle one step at a time and ensure you do all the I's and cross all the T's before moving onto the next one. There is no point getting ahead of yourself. Don't send out your resume if it is not ready. Likewise, don't apply for positions if you haven't set up a website or LinkedIn profile.

Start from the first chapter and then progress to the next making sure that all the boxes are ticked. This section will cement what you have learned in the earlier sections and give you the confidence you need to succeed in a coveted tech internship.

Succeeding at a no-name school

While a great school can open many doors, don't buy into the talk that if you fail to make the grade at a well-known college, your career won't take off. There are many success stories about people who prospered in their jobs, despite studying at a no-name school. There are even many successful individuals, who failed to get a degree at all. You shouldn't let any negative talk stand in your way – EVER!

As long as you follow the information we have laid out in the book, your school ultimately doesn't factor that high into the intern equation. If you are determined and driven, then you will be successful. We don't doubt that at all. Your college does not reflect who you are or what you will become.

Figure out your goal, put down the blueprint, take the steps you can control and chase your dreams. So, quit worrying about the fact that you didn't get accepted into the top ten schools in the country. Focus on where you are today, what is in your control, and what you need to do to make your resume absolutely blow them out of the water.

As you proceed throughout your career, the less relevant your degree and the school at which you studied becomes. As we talked about in this entire book, the skills and experience you bring to the table are the real factors. If you continue to learn and show commitment to your craft, you will land an internship regardless of any brand-name school you did or did not attend.

Your experience, i.e. the sum of your projects, your research, your clubs, your independent studies and your projects, will determine your track record and where you will go in the future. And those networking skills will come in handy too. Remember, you can't teach soft skills.

Considering how stressful it is to get into an elite school, you would think that it would have more sway. But, the truth of the matter is that while it does offer a small advantage, it is not necessarily a guarantee of success. Once a company sees how well you perform and gets an insight into your capabilities, you are set. And, as many hirers are learning, a student from a no-name school is quite often more determined that those students who attend the well-known college because they don't carry with them a sense of entitlement and understand the need for hard work.

When it comes down to it, employers value diversity, and it is this diversity that is beneficial to a company's success. Companies like to hire individuals from all walks of life because they understand that a variety of people will offer a broader perspective. Bottom line - work as hard as you can and represent yourself in the best manner possible. Use your education as a stepping stone to move onwards and upwards. You cannot go wrong!

Why your sub 3.0 GPA doesn't matter

There's a popular saying that goes along the lines of "'A' students work for 'B' students at companies founded by 'C' students". We touched upon the subject of Grade Point Average briefly in Chapter 2 – Getting Experience, however, it is worth bringing it up again. In the grand scheme of things, your GPA does not matter. Like the school you studied at, your GPA does not define you.

You are more than your grade point average – so much more in fact. And, in a year or two following graduation, no one will even care what your GPA was if you have corporate experience on your side. If you sit in an interview waiting to be asked what your GPA was in college, then you might be waiting a while! That question just isn't relevant in a working environment.

There are issues that are much more relevant to your employers such as your work ethic, your ability to follow instructions, and your communication abilities. So rather than putting more emphasis on your GPA, focus on your projects and your research – things that will build on your practical skills and make you stand out from the others who are vying for the same positions. These qualities will predict your job success more than your GPA ever will.

You can bet that a prospective employer will care more for the passionate individual with a 3.0 GPA who went out of the way to find opportunities to improve upon, and cement their skills through various research projects, over and above the student who sat and studied all night to get a 4.0 GPA.

Employers are seeking well-rounded individuals with real experience rather than just book experience. Your GPA is only one of many things they will take into consideration. A 3.0 GPA will not affect your hiring potential if you can demonstrate your positive mindset and your potential.

What to do if you're an international student, minority or disabled?

International Students

If you are an international student, you may be able to complete an internship provided you have the relevant visa and permission from either your school or the U.S. Citizenship and Immigration Services.

Curricular Practical Training (CPT)

If you are an international student on an F-1 student visa, a CPT may be issued before you finish your degree. CPTs are authorized for co-ops or internships which are considered necessary to your studies or learning. For your college to authorize CPT, you will need to have the relevant details printed on company letterhead before approval can be issued.

Your school may deem CPT not applicable to your studies, so seek advice from them at the outset to determine their specific regulations. If you undertake more than 12 months of CPT, your OPT (see below) may be reduced.

Optional Practical Training (OPT)

OPT is another form of temporary authorization permitting you to work, although it is usually considered following graduation. As all international students are eligible for at least one year of OPT after completion of their degree, you should have no problem obtaining permission for an internship at this time. Students who have completed degrees in a STEM-designated degree program are eligible to apply for a 17-month extension on their OPT. To be approved for OPT, you will need to complete Form-I765 and send it to the U.S. Citizenship and Immigration Services for approval.

Academic Training (AT)

Academic Training (AT) can also be given. It is a temporary authorization for students on a J-1 visa. AT can be used during the degree or following completion of the degree. If you have graduated with a bachelor's or master's degree, you are eligible for up to 18 months of work experience.

Those who have completed a doctoral degree are allowed an extension of up to 18 months (totaling no more than 36 months). If you are an exchange student on a J-1 visa, for every semester studied, you are eligible for up to four months of AT. Similar to the CPT, an offer must already be given by an employer before you apply. You will need to supply the job offer on company letterhead to your school, so they can approve your application.

Minority Students

There are many internships, fellowships, grants and sponsorship programs that can assist minorities in the search for their ideal job, particularly in the Science, Technology, Engineering and Mathematics (STEM) fields. In fact, some programs are available only to students of color or other minorities which are under-represented.

INROADS Internship Program

INROADS Internship Program is one such opportunity which helps students of color find internships in Fortune 1000 companies. You can learn more about them here: (www.inroads.org).

Management Leadership for Tomorrow (MLT) Program

MLT equips and emboldens high-achieving women and men from underrepresented communities – African

American, Latino/a and Native American – to realize their full potential, to make a mark and make a difference. You can learn more about them here: (www.ml4t.org).

Co-op/Internships and Summer Research Opportunities

An extensive list is published by Rochester Institute of Technology, and it is a great starting point for minority students. It lists positions from all over the country, so check it out to see whether any of them interest you.

Disabled Students

Most companies will be only too happy to accept disabled students for their internship provided they have the knowledge and the ability to do so. Students with disabilities – visible or non-visible - must learn to be vocal and open about their situation, particularly if it is going to impede their work in any way. An employer is required by law to make any reasonable adjustments, unless it causes undue hardship, to ensure that you are not placed at a significant disadvantage in comparison to the other candidates.

The reality is you have to be your own advocate and use your disability to educate companies on the benefits that come with hiring disabled students. It is only through education that employers are willing to make changes in the way they do business and become more accepting of those with a disability.

From a legal perspective, if you are a disabled student and attend an interview, you don't have to disclose your disability until you get the job. If you have a disability which does not affect the way you work or live, then you don't have to disclose it at all.

If your disability affects the way you work and live, then it may be wise to disclose it early on in the process so the company will be better prepared to answer some of the questions you may have. State your disability, how it affects you and whether you need any special amendments to be made. While you don't want your disability to hamper your hiring potential, it is solely up to you when you choose to tell your employer, your manager, your team and the colleagues you will be working alongside on a daily basis.

Entering an organization from a unique perspective such as yours is a tremendous educational prospect for the hiring company and it can teach them a lot about managing employees with disabilities in the future. You may have many strengths that they haven't even begun to imagine so don't be afraid to be vocal about all your assets and insights you can provide. You have much value to offer an employee, even if they are unable to see it yet.

Regardless of who you are or whether you have a disability, gaining an internship will strengthen your job prospects at the end of your studies. Therefore, it is worth sending out applications with passion and dedication, disability or not. Whether you choose to advise your prospective employer about your disability prior to the interview process, during the interview or after you have received a job offer will depend upon the severity of your disability and your personal situation.

Speak to the disability support office at your school to see whether they can add any extra insight to your case. The U.S. Equal Employment Opportunity Commission can provide much information on the legal ramifications of finding work with a disability. They can also give you advice if you believe that you have discriminated against during any process of the internship search.

Opportunities for Individuals with Disabilities

Here is an extensive list of opportunities for individuals with disabilities. Remember, if your disability affects the way you work, then it may be wise to disclose it early on in the process, but it definitely depends on a person-to-person basis.

- AAAS - EntryPoint! - Internship and full-time opportunities at various organizations such as Mayo Clinic, IBM, Merck, Lockheed Martin, etc.
- Lime Connect - Provides scholarships, internships, and networking at various technology firms, Goldman Sachs, Bloomberg, JPMorgan, Google, PepsiCo, IBM, Microsoft, etc.
- WRP - Full-time and internship opportunities for people with disabilities seeking government positions.

- <u>USBLN</u> – Provides mentoring, internships, full-time and networking opportunities for people with disabilities with large corporations (Northrop Grumman, Lockheed Martin, Verizon, JPMorgan, Boston Scientific, etc.)
- <u>Viscardi Center</u> – Provides mainly financial internships. Helps to connect individuals with disabilities to opportunities at insurance and banking institutions.
- <u>AAPD</u> - Partners with congressional summer opportunities, nonprofits, and government agencies around Washington, DC.
- <u>DO-IT</u> - Based out of University of Washington, focuses on providing mentoring, opportunities to students at a high school and college level.
- <u>COSD</u> - Internship opportunities for people with disabilities plus an annual conference.
- <u>Bender Consulting</u> - Career consulting service for individuals with disabilities.
- <u>Tapia Conference</u> - Computing conference scholarship for individuals with disabilities.
- <u>Project Starfish</u> – Career consulting service for individuals with disabilities.
- <u>AbleFlight</u> - Flying scholarships for individuals with physical disabilities.

Network your way to 500+ LinkedIn Connections

This may seem like an odd thing to do, but when it comes to LinkedIn, having over 500+ contacts will raise your profile and be a badge of legitimacy. To get there, however, the first thing you need to do is to ensure that your profile is thoroughly set up as per our detailed instructions in Chapter 3. When you have double checked it to ensure that there are no errors or missing information, it is time to start connecting with those you know and those you don't.

So, why 500? Well, whether you have 501 connections or 10,001, your LinkedIn connections will read no higher than 500+ (this may be subject to change in the future). 501 is essentially the magic number you need to hit before you can be taken seriously by recruiters and managers. And the more contacts you can get over this, the better, as some may drop off here and there. With a bit of concerted effort, you should be able to reach 500+ connections in just a few weeks.

If you haven't done so already, connect your email addresses and phone contacts so you can get in touch with everyone you know to date. That is the ideal start. Connect with everyone of value in your past circle and current circle to enable you to create a healthy looking account. Remember reaching out for connections before having a public-ready profile will defeat the purpose. You want a LinkedIn profile that people will be only too pleased to connect with – make it real and meticulously representative of your current position and your intended job search. At the moment your social circle may include fellow students, your teachers, your friends and any coworkers. Now widen your circle and connect with friends of those friends that are on the periphery of your contact list. Reach out and say hi and ask whether they would be interested in connecting with you.

Now, every time you meet someone new, add them to your network. Do it instinctively by sending a short note of introduction with every connection request. A note of introduction is necessary for every individual you connect to, unless you know them very well. It is polite, above all else, and it also acts as a reminder and lets people know who you are or where they met you.

Put your LinkedIn profile link on every bit of correspondence you send out so people will automatically click on your account when they see your link. Having others connect with you as a matter of course, will reduce the number of people you have to approach and can cut your workload down dramatically. Share your LinkedIn profile on Twitter and Facebook, and any other social media accounts that you have, and ask that people connect to your LinkedIn account. This will ensure you don't miss anyone on your list.

One of the vast benefits of LinkedIn is the groups that operate on there. Search and see which groups may be of interest to you. Locating relevant groups is easily done by searching for prominent keywords in the search box. Find a suitable group to begin with and then start networking. Then repeat.

Open up a dialogue with some of the people in the group and then once a conversation has started, send them a connect request. LinkedIn groups can be a great way to meet new people and widen your immediate circle within a short space of time. Consider it a shortcut to meeting people. If people see you interacting with their group, then they too will automatically reach out to you, particularly if you are providing value to the discussion. Don't be afraid to ask questions, comment on posts and like what others have to say. It will be to your benefit to join groups of all sizes. You can even consider starting your own group in the future if you believe you have a valuable niche that will help boost your profile.

Once you hit 250 connections, then 500+ should be well within arm's reach. You will need to spend on average, an hour or so each day, researching contacts and making connections. When you have more than 500 connections, then it is just a matter of updating your profile and chatting to those in your inner circle. And if you can arrange to meet up with as many people from your LinkedIn list in real life, even better, particularly in situations which will allow you to do even more networking.

When you have a substantial and sustainable network of 500+ contacts, then you can begin the internship search. Remember, however, it is the magic number to demonstrate that you want to be taken seriously in your job search. Therefore, aim for that before you start sending out those emails.

How to position yourself if you're not a Computer Science major

If you are looking for a tech internship without a major in computer science, it can still be done. Your focus, however, is to demonstrate the skills that you actually have and make those the feature of your resume. Try to take on technical work to show your commitment to the topic. Put your name down for side projects and research projects and list them on LinkedIn, your personal website and your resume.

Study new tech skills in your own time and list them on your resume. Outside learning is perfectly adequate for many smaller companies and startups, particularly ones that value dedication and potential above traditional learning routes.

Many internships don't necessarily require you to be a CS major as long as you have the majority of the soft skills to get the job done. Hard skills can be built on, even after you have landed an internship. Remember, never stop learning or showing your willingness to pick up more skills. There are tons of different tools online where you can earn free certificates and other ways to show competency. DataCamp.com, Microsoft Professional Program, and Codeacademy.com are all great resources to learn and grow.

Browse the internship advertisements and see what positions you like the sound of the most. Analyze the keywords and see where you fall short regarding your knowledge and experience. Then seek to fill in the gap. Your degree, like your GPA, will become less relevant the more real experience you get.

Finding housing and moving across the country

To make the daily commute to work, ideally, you want to find accommodation that is reasonably close to the company you will be interning for. Of course, the cost of rent will also need to factor into the equation. Once you know your salary, then you should be able to work out how much you will have left over for rent and other living expenses. Some organizations may be able to offer accommodation or a stipend to help cover rent, while others will leave the housing search and costs entirely up to you.

It can be challenging to find cheap accommodation in a new city, particularly when you are going to be located somewhere for only a short length of time. Therefore, it is wise to put your feelers out to see if any of your contacts know someone in the area who may be able to assist in your search, or better still, let you rent out their spare room. If it is a summer internship, then check with the local college as they often rent out temporary accommodation that is competitively priced. Ask your recruiter or contact at the company if there are any other interns that are going to be looking for housing as well.

If the company you are working for provides housing or suggestions, that is a great place to start. Most of the accommodation will also be furnished which will save a lot of stress and unnecessary expense. Searching Facebook for certain groups, such as nearby university housing subletting or housing within a given geographic location are always good ways to approach the housing game as well.

Here are some others that may also prove helpful in your search.

- Craigslist (www.craigslist.com)
- Student Housing (www.studenthousing.org)
- Apartment List (www.apartmentlist.com)
- Apartments (www.apartments.com)
- Easy Roommate (www.easyroommate.com)

These websites feature accommodations based all over the country, so you will need to scroll down to your city of choice and see what is available. There are also many websites that offer localized internship accommodation. Your careers center and the employer may even be able to provide some advice in this area. Failing that, browse the above list of websites and use Google to assist with the more area specific searches and see what you can find. There are certainly plenty of options out there, so try not to stress out about it unnecessarily.

If you are moving across the country for only a limited period of time, then you won't need to take everything you own. You will just need your clothes and a few personal belongings to get you started. Depending on your situation, you may need to find storage for your other belongings if you need to move out of your current accommodation. Otherwise, it is simply a case of packing a bag and either driving or catching a bus to your new home.

It is an exciting time for you, so take what you need to make yourself feel comfortable and relaxed.

How to move from one department to another at the same company

While an intercompany transfer from one department to another may not seem a big move at the outset, it can almost be likened to starting over again with a different company. You cannot presume that the work you did in one department will be similar to another or even that their methodology will be the same. Undoubtedly the new department may follow the same general overall ideology, but they can also operate very differently.

One positive thing which comes from a departmental transfer is you have virtually doubled your experience at the one company. It is a brilliant way to enhance your skills and expand your knowledge. And, even better, consider all those new faces that you will have the opportunity to network with in the future. Spend time getting to know your new colleagues, while at the same time nurturing your relationships with your previous contacts.

You may not have been anticipating a lateral move within the company, but it doesn't mean that you cannot make the most of the unexpected opportunity. Finish up everything which needs to be done in your current department; don't leave a big mess for someone else to sort out. Talk to your manager about their expectations on what you need to complete before you move. Otherwise, set tasks aside if the move is imminent and there appear to be time restrictions. This is not the time to slack off.

If the department has sourced another intern or employee to fill your position, then take the time to do a proper handover. Go through your duties and responsibilities to the best of your knowledge and leave written notes if it will help them with the role. Think back to when you started. What would have made the job transition more comfortable? What did you think was missing in your introduction? Explain to them that if they have any issues, then you are only a phone call or email away. After all, it's the polite thing to do!

When you are introduced to the new department, listen as carefully as if it was an entirely new company. Don't presume you know it already because you worked upstairs for a bit! Let them see your enthusiasm and your willingness to take on challenges and succeed. The chances are that your department has already heard a lot of positive things about you. Not it is all up to you to show them that the office gossip is correct on all counts.

Differences in the full-time job search

Sourcing a full-time job differs from an internship as you need to be committed to whatever decision you are going to make. Unlike an internship, accepting a full-time job with a company is considered a permanent move, so you need to take everything into account — new city, accommodation and long-term prospects. Of course, when we say permanent, we mean longer than a year or two, at least.

In today's workplace, employees are no longer expected to find work at one company and stay there until they retire. Employees will tend to stay as long as they are motivated and enjoying their work, then they will look for ways to better their skills and develop in their role. If there are seemingly limited options for advancement or change in their current employment, then they will move to another company.

Remember that many of your internships may lead to full-time jobs. So, if you have nurtured your contacts and kept in touch with them throughout your studies, hopefully, you can minimize the actual job search to find a full-time position.

If this is not the case, then you will need to hit the job boards just as you did the internships. Make sure that your resume, website and LinkedIn profile are up to date. Personalize your cover letter and resume just as you did with your intern applications. Reach out to the recruiters and keep checking all the sites until you find something you like the sound of. Then you can send out your cover letters and resumes, and hope for the best.

Use the following websites to help you get started:

- Glassdoor (www.glassdoor.com)
- Indeed (www.indeed.com)
- LinkedIn (www.linkedin.com)
- Monster (www.monster.com)

Optimize your career for success

As you will have undoubtedly discovered in your internship search, the world of tech careers can be very competitive. Determining what makes you unique, and working hard to learn as much as possible, will have proven beneficial to date. But how can you take what you have learnt and use it to optimize your career for long-term success?

Here is our list of the top 12 things to do to keep your eyes on the prize.

1. Continue learning

Never stop learning or wanting to improve your skills. You are an investment, so any time or effort it takes to upgrade your skills through online or offline training, it is worth it. Stay ahead of your peers by continuously looking for options to update your skills and always be on the lookout for new ways to learn.

2. Understand your goals

As you gain more work experience, you will get to know yourself better. You will realize what makes you happy and what kind of career you are interested in seeking in the future. To be ultra-clear on where you want to be in one year, two years or five years, write it down. Think about realistic targets which will help you meet these goals.

3. Find a mentor

If you can find a mentor who can guide you in your career choices, even better. Identify someone in the field who you respect. Ask them if they would like to act as a mentor and make suggestions or provide help with any issues you face in your career. Chances are whatever you are going through, they have been there, and they can offer helpful ways to move forward. There is no need to make unnecessary mistakes if someone can steer you in the right direction.

4. Improve your communication skills

Having excellent communication skills is imperative to your long-term career success. Practice your skills or even take a course in learning how to communicate effectively. Being able to listen attentively without interrupting, and speaking well using tactics such as persuasion and influence, will propel your career forward. Regardless of your future career choice, improving your communication skills will open up many doors.

5. Network

Networking is something we have mentioned numerous times throughout this book and with good reason. It is important that you continue to build on your network and nurture the contacts you already have. Always seek out ways to broaden your social circle and accept any invitations that will take you somewhere new or allow you to meet new people.

6. Take any feedback to heart

Any direction you are given in terms of feedback and appraisals should be listened to and followed. If you need to improve in areas, then do it. If you are given recommendations, then take them on board. This advice is offered free by those in the know who care about your career and your future.

7. Avoid situations which will affect your career negatively

To maintain the respect of your manager and peers, it is best to stay away from office gossip at all times. If you hear someone gossiping about another coworker try to a) change the subject or b) walk away. Don't let anyone else's terrible attitude brings your own reputation down. It is always best to avoid talking negatively about your employer or any of your colleagues, regardless of how unhappy you are in your current position. If you have issues with your company or another colleague, then speak to them directly.

8. Position yourself as an expert in your field

Know your facts. If you want to be taken seriously in your career, then become an asset to the company and your field. Go above and beyond what needs to be done and set yourself up as an expert. You might want to consider adding a blog to your website and discussing valuable aspects of your career from a general perspective. By giving back in this way, you can put yourself in a mentoring position to others.

9. Take on extra responsibility

Find ways to take on extra responsibility over and above your average day to day tasks. Show your employer that you are eager to learn and that you want to be a valued member of the team. If you don't have enough work, then ask for more. Always try to add extra value to your efforts by coming up with new ideas that will positively affect the company. Demonstrating your initiative will provide a much-needed boost to your career and make sure you get noticed by all the right people.

10. Maintain your passion

It can sometimes be difficult to maintain your enthusiasm for the role when you are overworked and overtired. During these periods, remind yourself what you love about the job and focus on your passion that got you into the rewarding career in the first place. If people see you are happy, confident and positive, regardless of how mundane your duties are, then people will naturally want to be around you and support your growth. Understanding how you fit into the big picture is a learning experience in itself. Any small task that you do will enable everyone else to function well around you. Even if you don't feel it, you are helping your team and your company succeed.

11. Always be a team player

Being able to get along with and work well with others is necessary. Always be willing to pull your weight in group activities and show that you value being a respected member of the team. Demonstrate your reliability and ability to adapt well to new situations. Do more than is asked of you and always be committed to the end goals. These traits will get you a long way in your career.

12. Work smarter

There are always ways you can improve the manner in which you work. If you missed the mark today, what can you do better tomorrow? There is no point beating yourself up about it if things don't go your way. Take a wide-angled approach and look at ways you could improve. How could you do better? Constantly take notes and check your facts, so you don't waste your time having to redo a task.

It pays to take a moment at the end of each day to plan what is on your to-do list for the following day. It may change in the natural scheme of things, but having a rough plan will ensure you give yourself enough time to get things done.

Taking full advantage of the internship

An internship is the best way to see how you will operate in a full-time position. Follow our tips to ensure you make the most of every opportunity. If you want to see your internship convert to a full-time job in the future, then avoid these common mistakes.

1. Be over familiar or too casual

Even if the company code is casual, it pays to avoid being too relaxed about your internship. Always act professionally and with respect for your colleagues and peers. Show them that you want to improve your position and move up that corporate ladder. Keep your personal life separate and avoid discussing issues about your home life unless otherwise asked. Maintain an air of professionalism at all times.

2. Constantly being late

Always arrive to work on time, avoid taking long lunches and stay until the end of the workday. If you do need to leave early or come in late, for any reason, then let the company know well in advance. If you are always calling in sick and failing to complete your work in a timely fashion, it will be noted on your file. Don't make a habit of it.

When it comes to managing your time inside the office, always work to deadline and avoid submitting your work late. Prioritize your tasks to honor those deadlines without any excuse.

3. Refuse to do menial tasks

In any job, there are always duties that you may not want to carry out. But, in order to fulfill your job description, unfortunately, it is necessary to do them. Many dull and menial jobs are offered to interns. So do them with a smile on your face regardless of how much you hate them.

We understand that no one wants to be lumped with the filing or the photocopying, but the reality is someone has to do it – so it might as well be you. Once you get the less than fulfilling jobs out of the way, then perhaps you can approach your manager for a challenge that you can really sink your teeth into.

4. Dress inappropriately

Avoid dressing too casual for your role. If you believe you don't have anything appropriate for the position, then go shopping and find some smart dress wear to suit the occasion. You don't want to overdress for the role or subsequently underdress. If you are unsure, then ask about the dress policy before you start and head straight to the store to make sure you are well-prepared. First impressions do count, so make it a good one!

5. Forget to ask for feedback

Failure to ask for feedback or constructive criticism is a failure to learn. Always check in with your managers to see what you could improve, and where exactly you should be aiming for. Feedback on any role is important, and it is a valuable way to learn how to develop your skills and performance levels.

6. Ignore your relationships

You need to spend the appropriate amount of time nurturing your relationships in a professional manner. Socialize with your coworkers and always maintain your contacts once the internship is over. Instead of spending all the time at your desk, get up and speak to people. Get to know them, even if you don't work with them directly. Ask others to go for a coffee or have lunch with you and make a real effort to get to know more about them. You never know what doors they may be able to open up in the future.

7. Failure to use the available resources

You will find that most companies will subscribe to specific journals and magazines. Find out who receives them and see if you can be added to the reading list. Explain at the outset that you are very keen to learn and that you want to be included in any potential learning opportunities which may arise during your time in the office. This goes for any applicable staff training opportunities as well.

8. Take your internship for granted

Many interns believe that once they have landed the position, then they can use it as an opportunity to slack off. Think seriously about your actions which can affect your career choices in the long-term and then act accordingly. One black mark against your name for whatever reason can ruin your career, and it will definitely hinder your job choices with that company in the future.

9. Work yourself to the ground

Depending on the company you are working for, you may find that you are working too hard or too long. Prioritize your workload and avoid overextending yourself. While you do want to make a good impression, pretending that you are okay working from 7 AM to 7 PM every day will lead to stress and burnout. Pace yourself and learn to say no when appropriate. No one will think any the less of you if you leave on time to catch up on some rest and relaxation. You are no good to the organization if you fall ill through overwork.

10. Ignore company processes and policies

Every company is different and not paying attention to specific processes or policies can lead to issues. Watch and see how others carry out their task and follow suit. You may need to adjust the way you do things to meet the expectations and goals of the business. Demonstrate your flexibility to do that, and you will always be taken seriously. Take notes where necessary, so you don't forget things. Frequently having to ask how to do things over and over again will not help you any.

Remember that you may not be 100% happy with all of the aspects of your internship or even the specific company that took a chance on you, but that is no reason to slack off or act unprofessionally. Bear in mind that you are there for a limited period and try to learn as much as you can. Turn it into a rewarding experience rather than a punishment. And, if you do realize that it is not the company for you, just think yourself fortunate that you aren't working there as a full-time employee.

Online Resources

We hope you have enjoyed our vault of successful resumes, cover letters, interview questions and answers. For ease, we have listed the information in one place so you can access it as you need to. We wish you the best of luck in your internship search.

- Resume Example
- Resume Template
- Cover Letter Example
- Cover Letter Template
- Interview Preparation Template
- Questions to Ask
- LinkedIn Profile Example
- Opportunity Template
- Elevator Pitch Template
- Cold Email Template
- Negotiation Articles

All Resources:

(www.internblueprint.com/resources)

Notes

About the Author

Ray Parker is from Mill Creek, Washington. He is a learner, chemical engineer, rocket scientist and author who has wants to help. Ray graduated from Rensselaer Polytechnic Institute with a degree in chemical engineering and Smartly, an online MBA degree program.

He currently lives in the greater Seattle region. Visit him at www.rayokadaparker.com.

Made in the USA
Lexington, KY
18 August 2018